Corruption
Core - Option

Edwin Masih

Editor: Terrie Scott

ISBN 13:978-1978005570
ISBN 10:1978005571

Printed in the United States of America

Dedication

This book is a dedication to every man and woman who has lost their dreams, hopes, future, families, and lives in a struggle against corruption. They had what it takes to be a successful individual, but they never compromised their core values.

"Cowards bow before corruption,

the courageous stand up against corruption."

Acknowledgments

Making an effort to achieve is human nature. It is our attitude that teaches us that nothing is impossible, that I can do everything; the sky is the limit, or whether one is born with a finite skill set. It doesn't matter how talented, skillful, brainy, or gifted we are, we always need guidance, inspiration, motivation, and support to reach our destination. I am not hesitant to display my gratitude to each person who has inspired me to use my gift of writing, the power of expression to serve humanity.

I acknowledge my family for their relentless support and for enabling me to bring my thoughts onto the printed page. My efforts would be useless without the inspiration of my mother Alice and father Rashid, who taught me to trust my gut. My lovely wife Joyce has stood beside me for every step of life. Her love keeps my heart clean and corruption free. My daughters Abhishika and Anmol taught me how to value different perspectives. My son Samuel inspired me and taught me that without hard work and endurance we can't make our place. It is a long race! My brother Gulshan and sister Rajkumari always remind me that patience is a virtue!

Dr. James, a neuro-surgeon, recognized my hidden talent of speaking my mind through writing. Dr. Gary Johnson motivates me to use the power of truth. Truth prevails! A special thanks to Terrie Scott, a writer who guided me in compiling and publishing this book. There is also a long list of family members and friends who have contributed, directly and indirectly, spurring me on write about my ideas, and without their support and inspiration I would have been unable to send this message to millions! Thank you to the Almighty!

Introduction

An Indian joke caught my attention with the title "Financial Management without MBA." The joke goes this way. A beggar got a one-hundred-rupee bill, and he went to dine out at an elite restaurant. After wining and dining, the waiter brought a payment check of 3000 Indian rupees. The beggar looked at the ticket and refused to pay the bill. The manager called the police and handed the beggar over to the police. As soon as both stepped outside the restaurant, the beggar slid 100 rupees to the cop and cop released him without asking a question. It is called "Financial Management without MBA." Although the joke tells how the beggar was clever and used the loop hole of the system, it shows the crisp picture of a corrupt world we live in.

We don't have to be a rocket scientist to figure out why administration jobs are handed over to people who don't have skills, ability, and qualification. Why don't intelligent, brilliant, and hardworking people move up the ladder of their career while people with connections do? Why the research committees pick a compromised product or a theory over the better one? Why are drugs free floating in the street? Although there is always an option to pick a reasonable person for a position, support a credible theory, stand for the ethical and moral issue and keep the deal visible, corruption can turn everything upside down in a blink. It makes no sense, despite the availability of modern tools, technology, and resource why we keep failing to stop corruption.

There has been a lot of evidence that reveals that corruption is not a new subject in the discussion of the human society. But quite recently, it has been the subject of hot public debates and the focal point of many governments in the past decade. Does it mean that corruption has increased in scope and reach in the last ten years? Or is it because it has just gotten more attention than what used to be the case? The scale tilts to the former. Corruption has become more pervasive in today's society. It has grown by leaps and bounds, and the fact that the world is increasingly becoming globalized hasn't helped matters.

Actionable steps can be taken to ensure that corruption is reduced to the barest minimum, but the fight against corruption and corrupt practices is not something that should be left to the state or one sector alone to take care of. The reason is that the state in one way or the other still creates a breeding ground for corruption. Corruption has been the subject of hot public discussions and the focal point of many governments in the past decade. But corruption is not new as a weakness of the human society. Does it now mean then that corruption has increased in scope and reach in the last decade?

Corruption has become more pervasive in today's society. This book looks at corruption from a holistic perspective. Corruption in government sparks a debate, but an attempt has been made to delve deeper into the other manifestations of corruption Such as, why it happens? How it is being propagated? What other areas of social life has it permeated? And, what actionable solutions should be taken to stunt its growth?

It is worthy to note that corruption cannot be eliminated. Zero corruption cannot be achieved, but zero tolerance for corruption is what should be a slogan of every individual and citizen. A fight against corruption is a civic duty and collective responsibility. It is the duty of everyone to take up arms against corruption. Anti-corruption strategies should also be on the political agenda of every ruling party. It should not only be there on the agenda, but it should also be actively pursued. It is only when this is done that the government can adequately cater for the needs of its electorates.

But fighting corruption requires an understanding of its dynamics: its propagation, reach, and termination. This book has taken a close look at all of these and has proffered solutions that are effective in putting an end to the destructive action of corruption in our social and political society.

Chapter One

The Rise and Rise of Corruption

Quite recently, especially in the 1990s, the phenomenon called corruption has greatly attracted attention. In developed and developing countries, great or small, economically-diverse or mono-product, multicultural or not, many governments have been pulled down with many prominent leaders including presidents forced out of their offices, and, in many severe cases, the entire ruling classes replaced.

The world is not new to corruption. For instance, in mythology, Dante punished bribers by banishing them to hell. In plays by William Shakespeare, the renowned writer and playwright, corruption was many times featured as a theme. Even in the American Constitution, which is over 200 years old, bribery is explicitly mentioned as a crime that could get an American president impeached. However, the kind of attention that corruption has gotten in recent years has been unprecedented. For instance, Financial Times announced 1995 as the year of corruption in its last editorial for the same year.

Now, this makes one wonder, why all this sudden attention to corruption and its practices? Does this mean that we are more corrupt today than we used to be? Or does it mean that more attention is being paid to something that used to exist but is largely ignored, although not totally? There is no clear answer to these, but there are plausible reasons which could attempt to explain why corruption has been basking in the limelight in recent years.

First of all, the end of the Cold War signaled an end to the kind of hypocrisy that made the government of industrialized nations turn a blind eye to the high levels of corruption in many other countries particularly in developing countries such as Zaire, Senegal, and Sierra Leone. What is obtained is that developed countries overlook apparently high levels of corruption in developing countries where they benefited.

Secondly, more countries today now practice democracy, which has made the media free and more active in informing the people about the activities of their political leaders. In countries such as Nigeria and Russia, the media has been very outspoken about corruption in the face of this new freedom.

Thirdly, increased internet penetration, global use of mobile phones, and consequently globalizations have brought more people together, which means citizens of countries with high corruption rate can now voice their concern and seek the help of those from other countries that have managed to keep their corruption level low.

Also, the number of Non-Governmental Organizations (NGO) such as Transparency International has increased in recent times, which means that more people are now reporting and publicizing corrupt practices and putting in a lot of efforts to ensure that the anti-corruption movement takes hold in many countries. Many international financial institutions and organizations have also developed anti-corruption sensitization programs and schemes to provide the minimal demand for, and supply of corrupt practices in the financial sector.

Moreover, today, there is a greater dependence on the market in the making of critical economic decisions than there used to be. This means that efficiency has become the watchword, and any distortion by corruption would get serious attention.

Finally, the developed countries including the United States government have played a lot of roles in bringing the war against corruption to the doorsteps of many countries and international organizations. Many policy makers in America have brought forward the argument that their inability to pay bribes in countries where it is the norm has made them lose a lot in foreign deals. US laws forbid the payment and receipt of bribes whether at home or abroad. Therefore, the law doesn't see the payment of bribes as a cost that can be taxed since it is illegitimate.

In the United States, the newly-elected President is hoping to fulfill his election promise on his war against corruption in Washington. On January 20, 2017, Donald John Trump at the age of 70 became the 45th president of the United States of

America and the wealthiest to have ever contested and won in an election. That will continue to be the fodder for discussions and political argument for decades to come.

In a statement posted on his website, on October 18th, 2016, at www.donaldjtrump.com, just a few weeks from his election reads:

"There is another major announcement I am going to make today as part of our pledge to drain the swamp in Washington. If I am elected President, I will push for a Constitutional Amendment to impose term limits on all members of Congress.

Decades of failure in Washington and decades of special interest dealing must come to an end. We have to break the cycle of corruption, and we have to give new voices a chance to go into government service. The time for Congressional term limits has arrived...

"If we let the Clinton Cartel run this government, history will record that 2017 was the year America lost its independence. We will not let that happen. It is time to drain the swamp in Washington, D.C. That is why I am proposing a package of ethics reforms to make our government honest once again.

First: I am going to institute a 5-year ban on all executive branch officials lobbying the government after they leave government service.

Second: I am going to ask Congress to institute its 5-year ban on lobbying by former members of Congress and their staffs.

Third: I am going to expand the definition of the lobbyist, so we close all the loopholes that former government officials use by labeling themselves consultants and advisors when we all know they are lobbyists.

Fourth: I am going to issue a lifetime ban against senior executive branch officials lobbying on behalf of a foreign government.

Fifth: I am going to ask Congress to pass a campaign finance reform that prevents registered foreign lobbyists from raising money for the American election..."

Newly-released FBI documents revealed just how deep the corruption goes. The under-Secretary of State, Patrick Kennedy, illegally pressured the FBI to un-classify emails from Hillary's [Trump's running mate & wife of former president, Bill Clinton] illegal server. In other words, the State Department was trying to cover-up Hillary's crime of sending classified information to a server our enemies could easily access.

The FBI documents show that Patrick Kennedy requested altering classification as part of a *"quid pro quo."* Is it a felony corruption? Under-Secretary Kennedy needs to resign.

In its 2016 Corruption Perception Index, Transparency International noted that *"The interplay of corruption and inequality also feeds populism. When traditional politicians fail to tackle corruption, people grow cynical. Increasingly, people are turning to populist leaders who promise to break the cycle of corruption and privilege. This is likely to exacerbate – rather than resolve – the tensions that fed the populists' surge in the first place."*

This could probably explain why Hilary Clinton, a former US senator and Secretary of State with more political experience and popularity vote, still lost the election to inexperienced Trump. A great lesson to be learned!

Chapter Two

Understanding Corruption

The Panama Papers is one of the biggest leaks of offshore records and financial documents. It exposes an array of corruption and financial crime on a global scale. Released in 2016, the leak involving over 11 million records, reveals how a global industry of law firms and giant financial institutions sell financial secrecy to public officials & politicians, fraudsters, celebrities, sports stars, as well as billionaires. It is one of the biggest leaks in history surpassing in size the US diplomatic cables released by WikiLeaks under the leadership of Julian Assange. The Panama Papers is a result of an investigation by the International Consortium of Investigative Journalists, the German newspaper Süddeutsche Zeitung and over 100 news organizations across the world.

The leaked documents reveal the offshore holdings of 12 current and former presidents. It also exposes how people linked to Russian President Vladimir Putin, hid almost $2 billion using shell companies and banks. The documents also bring to light the details of the hidden financial dealings of 128 politicians across different countries around the world. For instance, the leak contained documents showing offshore companies under the control of the prime ministers of Iceland and Pakistan, including that of the King of Saudi Arabia and the children of the president of Azerbaijan. It also contains a list of at least 33 people, including companies that blacklisted because of their dealings with drug lords, terrorist organizations, and rogue nations. In fact, one of the documents showed that one of those blacklisted companies supplied fuel for the aircraft that the Syrian government used in killing its citizens.

The data spanning over 40 years from 1977 through 2015, chronicles how dark money flows through the global financial system, giving birth to crimes and robbing national treasuries of their tax revenues.

Now, many of the services provided by offshore companies are legal, if they are used by law-abiding citizens. But in the Panama Papers leak, documents reveal that banks, law firms, and other overseas players most of the time do not follow legal requirements. These legal requirements ensure that their clients are not meddling in criminal businesses, tax evasion, or some political corruption. In many instances, the document reveals that the offshore middlemen have shielded themselves and their clients by manipulating official records or concealing shady transactions.

The Panama Papers reveal that major banks are the ones propelling the creation of difficult-to-trace companies in the British Virgin Islands and other offshore financial havens. The files show that over 16,000 paper companies were listed by clients who want to keep their finances secret, including those created by big companies such as UBS and HSBC. The records also indicate a pattern of secret maneuvers by banks, companies, and people connected to the Russian President Vladimir Putin. The paper reveals that offshore companies linked to this network moving money in deals as high as $200 million at once. The associates of the Russian president disguised payments and tampered with the dates of documents. The leaked records came from a relatively unknown law firm in Panama named Mossack Fonseca hence the tag, The Panama Papers. Mossack Fonseca has branches in Hong Kong, Miami, Zurich, and in over 30 places around the world.

In Iceland for instance, the leaked documents show that during the country's financial stress, the Prime Minister David Gunnlaugsson and his wife possessed an offshore firm which contained millions of dollars wrapped in Icelandic bonds.

It doesn't end there. The Panama Papers includes other details about serious corruption scandals from England's infamous gold heist, to the broad bribery within FIFA, the world football governing body. In the case of FIFA, The Panama Papers showed that the law firm of Juan Pedro Damiani (who is a member of FIFA ethics committee) conducted business with three associates who had been indicted in the 2015 FIFA bribery scandal. The trio of FIFA's former president, Eugenio Figueredo, Hugo and Mariano Jinkis were all allegedly involved in the payment and receipt of bribes to secure broadcast rights for Latin-American soccer games. The records reveal that an offshore company connected to the Jinkises and seven other companies with links to Figueredo is represented by the law firm of Damiani in Uruguay.

Soccer legend, Lionel Messi, was also named in the documents. The papers revealed that Messi and his father were owners of a Panama company known as Mega Star Enterprises Inc. The multiple award-winning soccer star has been battling a tax evasion case in Spain where he is currently playing for the Spanish giant, Barcelona FC.

The definition of corruption varies, and there is no universally accepted and comprehensive definition of corruption. There have been a lot of attempts to find a unifying definition, but all these attempts have encountered legal, criminological, and even political bottlenecks. Many options that have been considered include not defining corruption as well as proposals, listing the specific forms under which corruption occurs and can be addressed. The proposals to make corruption a criminal offense consisted of specific offenses or group of offenses which depend on who is committing the offense (whether they are public officials or not), where the offense occurs (whether it is a cross-border activity or foreign officials were involved, and unlawful monetary/political gain).

At the deliberations of the United Nations Convention which began in 2002, specific forms of corruption were defined and understood. Many countries have also made attempts to criminalize these forms of corruption, while many others feel that it is much better to use regulatory and civil-law controls.

Despite all of this, the popular definition of corruption in many texts is, *"any dishonest act or a breach of ethical conducts by someone entrusted with authority to achieve personal gains."* Corruption occurs in many forms including bribery, misappropriation of funds, and financial embezzlement. In government, political corruption can occur when a political office holder uses the power given to him by the electorate for personal benefits.

The discussion of corruption is made difficult as it is a hidden societal phenomenon. For instance, one of the most common manifestations of corruption is bribery. When corruption takes place, both parties involved, act in exchange for their gains and do all they can to keep their transaction hidden. This secrecy makes it very difficult to analyze the extent corruption has penetrated in the economy and social life of citizens. Besides, there is the issue of cultural difference. What may be permissible in one culture might not be the same in another. What may be considered as a "friendly gift" in one culture may be regarded as a breach of ethics in another culture. What is seen as a friendly act in Mozambique may be considered misbehavior in the United States because of the cultural difference.

In fact, in some cases, what is acceptable at a particular hour of the day might be considered as inappropriate at another time. This complication is even taken a step further because many don't take accountability seriously. In many developing countries, such as those of Western Africa, there are still some significant scores of citizens who do not blame or hold public officials accountable for their corrupt acts. Many of these people also allege that those in higher authority ask to be bribed or give the opportunity to be bribed, and they have no other choice than to comply.

Many givers offer the excuse that "It is simply the system and they have no choice than to comply because if they don't, they risk losing a potential advantage." The real question is: Who is to blame for corruption? The person who demands or the person who bribes? In 20th century Pakistan, it is considered a general practice to increase every invoice written out for the government by seven percent. This increment is to account for the gift offered to a public official or politician in exchange for the privilege to supply a service or product to the government. So, it is only normal that even after this seven percent increase, there are other additional payments made, and these are considered as appreciation for the privilege obtained.

In every society, the ideology of which a public official is open to the receipt of "gifts" in exchange for a favor is something that is sometimes public or intuitive. This favor may be for the consideration of a juicy employment in the organization, or for the assignment of a contract, scholarship, or work. In some cases, it now becomes the task of the favor-seeker to look for this official whom everyone knows can be bought; someone everybody knows is susceptible to circumvent due process for the receipt of a gift. Therefore, reputation is also a factor in the discussion of corruption. Some officials or institutions will never be approached for this proposition as their stance is well-known to potential bribes. In the same regard, some businesses also are well-known for not offering bribes to anyone. These kinds of activities do so at a lesser risk of falling victims to corruption, which is one of the problems bribery brings with it.

Corruption is more than just a business problem. The fact that people who engage in it struggle to keep their acts secret is enough reason to prove that it is also an ethical problem. It also shows that those who do it know that it is an improper behavior. Beyond that, corruption is even seen as a behavioral problem, with many people referring to it as a sinful act and wrongdoing and one that should be corrected through a personal reform.

For instance, Transparency International (TI), an international anti-corruption watchdog defines corruption as "bad business practice"— a definition based on a moral judgment. Corruption transcends economic depths. It is not enough to only see corruption as an economic problem because this ignores all other facets of corruption that makes a corruption-free society very important for all, both rich and poor. A definition based on economics alone also overlooks the fact that corruption always occurs within a social context. In companies, where transparency is not practiced, where observance is not given priority, laws will be broken, and a structural problem will be created.

Emphasizing the evils of corruption is aimed at improving individual and personal behavior.

Chapter Three

Forms of Corruption

Corruption exists on many different levels.

1. Petty Corruption

Petty corruption is a form of corruption that occurs on a relatively small scale, involving a very few number of people. It may take the form of providing small favors to friends, families, and even acquaintances by circumventing due process. This is very common in public offices such as police stations and registration offices. Often, due process is bypassed when a "small" bribe is paid, or the promise of a return favor is made. Petty corruption usually happens between government officials and ordinary citizens especially when these citizens are trying to gain access to basic goods and services in public places such as hospitals, schools, immigration offices and other government agencies.

2. Systemic Corruption

Systemic corruption is one that occurs as a result of the weakness of an organization or system whether private or public, but it is most commonly found in the public system. It is different from individuals acting corruptly in the system.

Systemic corruption is a process-enabled corruption. For instance, a lack of transparency culture, low pay, monopoly, and discretionary powers in a system all encourage corruption. Examples of systemic corruption are financial misappropriations, bribery, and extortion.

3.   Grand Corruption

Another form of corruption is Grand Corruption which exists at the highest levels of government and involves a large-scale subversion of a country's established political, legal, and economic system. This form of corruption is commonly found in countries where the system of government is a military dictatorship or authoritarianism. It is also found in democratic climates too, especially in countries where ineffective policing of corruption is ineffective. In many countries, having three arms of government (legislative, judiciary and executive) is an attempt to ensure that power is sufficiently shared and independent services are being provided in such a way that the entire system of government is less liable to fall victim to the holds of grand corruption. Since great corruption happens at the highest level of government, government policies are twisted to favor the political elites, thereby negatively affecting the proper functioning of the state.

Many people often find petty corruption more irritating than grand corruption as they are directly affected. People frown at having to pay extra for a public service that should ordinarily be free. In the lowest cadre of organizations, petty corruption is most rampant while at the uppermost level, grand corruption reigns supreme. It often makes hard for high-ranking officials to act against petty corruption by subordinates, especially since these subordinates see that their superiors are constantly lining their pockets with big gifts.

What Causes Corruption?

Corruption is connected with the activities of the government especially when it comes to its discretionary powers. Therefore, one can be tempted to think that taking down the government is a solution to taking down corruption. It may seem like a good solution on the surface, but it isn't on closer observation. For any civilized society to function and even function properly, there has to be a government in place. For instance, countries like Canada, Sweden, Netherlands, and Finland where there are insufficient levels of corruption. Even the perception of it has some of the largest public sectors measured as shares of tax revenue or government spending in GDP. What this means is that taking down or reducing the size of the government is not the solution to corruption. Instead, what could be done is isolating those functions of government that creates the breeding ground for corruption and dealing with them.

This leads to the discussion of:

1. **Regulations and Authorizations**

The governments of many countries, especially those of developing countries, carry out its role through the enforcement of rules and regulations. It is also the government's function to issue licenses, permits, and different authorizations as at when needed. Activities like opening a business and sustaining its operations, borrowing of funds, investments, owning a car and keeping it on the road, building a house and maintaining it, obtaining forex for business, getting a national identity card or passport, travelling out of the country, to mention a few, are the state's duties.

The fact that government performs these regulatory and authorizations functions confers some supreme power on government officials who are employed to oversee these functions. Government officials can use their positions to demand bribes from citizens or companies who need these licenses and permits.

Bureaucracy in regulations and authorizations also ensures that time and efforts are both wasted. Therefore, officials may delay the issuance of a license for months, something which ordinarily should not take a week if "expedition fees" are not paid. Other times, citizens themselves might offer a bribe to expedite the process.

2. Taxation

Corruption can arise from taxation, if the laws are not quite clear and if they require that the taxpayers and tax inspectors make frequent contacts. To explain further when:

- The rules on taxation are not clear enough and are open to different interpretations to the extent that the taxpayers need the assistance of the tax inspectors;

- The process of tax payment requires that taxpayers and reviewer make frequent contacts;

- The salaries of tax inspectors are small;

- There is only slight punishment for corruption tax inspectors;

- The procedures for tax collection and remittance are not transparent enough;

- Tax inspectors have too many discretionary powers in areas like tax breaks, incentives, litigation, tax liabilities, etc.;

- The state has weak control over tax administration and administrators, which is why corruption creeps into the system and grow to become a major source of worry in the administration of tax.

3. Expenditure plans

Corruption can occur from the spending decision of a government or public decision. For instance, investment projects are high targets for corrupt public officials. When there is too much discretionary power in the hands of high-level officials, public spending decisions can become much distorted, both in size and in composition due to corruption. Sometimes, public officials create public projects to provide themselves with opportunities to enrich their pocket either through "commissions" from the project or "budget-padding" (where the original cost of the project is inflated). For these reasons, projects are not always executed based on merit, especially when a cost-benefit analysis is involved. Rather projects are executed because they will suit the officials.

Procurement spending is another area of state expenditure that becomes a target of corruption. It is also not uncommon to find extra-budgetary accounts in many countries. While some of them may be set up for legitimate reasons such as pension funds, a lot are set up to minimize the political and administrative control over the resources. And, since they do not directly go into the budget, they are therefore less transparent making them susceptible to hijacking by public officials.

In all of these cases, the lack of transparency and effective institutional controls give rise to corruption.

4. Unchecked discretionary decisions

In many countries, the powers of many public officials are not always spelled out clearly. So, they end up using a lot of discretion in making important decisions. This discretionary authority often encourages high-level corruption especially in areas such as:

• Decisions over the use of government-owned lands, for instance, mining and logging. There have always been cases of corruption relating to the awarding of oil mining licenses and permission to cut down trees in public-owned forests, in several countries;

• Decisions involving the authorization of foreign investments that are often connected with domestic interests, hence leading to the development of a monopoly power with the privileged investor;

• Decision relating to the sale of national assets;

• Decisions on the privatization of national goods and the regulatory conditions involved in it.

All these decisions are usually worth so much to many individuals and organizations. It is only normal that many will attempt to use this discretionary power loophole to their advantage by paying bribes or leveraging on personal relationships with the public officials. If the civil servant's wage is low, then they are more susceptible to receiving the bribe the next time.

5. Public sector wages

There is no denying the fact that low pay makes corruption all the more tempting. Many countries such as Argentina and Peru have tried in recent times to reduce corruption particularly in important and touchy areas such as customs, law enforcement, and taxation by increasing the monthly pay of employees in these sectors. They have also tried by increasing salary differentials in these sectors so that productivity and honesty can be encouraged. In many countries, particularly in developing ones, there have been calls for the wages of politicians to be slashed to make corruption less attractive. Nigeria is a prime example of this. Politicians and lawmakers in Nigeria are amongst the highest paid in the world, with a high school educated House of Representative member earning more than 50 times the salary of an average industrial worker.

6.   Inappropriate penalties

While in theory, stiff penalties tend to reduce the number of corrupt practices. Everything being equal, in the real world, only relatively few people get punished for corruption charges irrespective of the extent of the crime. Moreover, there seems to be a gap (except in a tiny number of countries) between the punishment prescribed by the law and that which is imposed. Those imposed tend to be milder than what is statutorily mandated.

Many times, there are legal, political, and administrative impediments to the prosecution of offenders to the full extent of the law. Incontrovertible evidence and due process are examples of legal hurdles that stand in the way of prosecution. Besides that, the judges who will rule on such cases may also be compromised. They become politically biased or become accessible to bribery so that legal proceedings can be frustrated and cases will be eventually struck out. For all of these reasons, penalties may not be effective in stemming the tide of corruption, particularly when it is politically motivated. In the end, these attitudes lead to a high tolerance level for small acts of corruption that can grow over time to become bigger and grander.

7. Institutional controls

One of the most effective ways of checking corruption is to set up ant-corruption institutions that will monitor government and private sector activities to ensure that financial transparency in observed. The structure and operation vary from country to country while in many they are either still ineffective or non-existent.

Many countries such as Singapore, Nigeria, Hong Kong, Uganda to mention a few, have set up anti-corruption commissions with the responsibility of following up and prosecuting corruption. However, some of these commissions have not been so effective because they are not completely independent, do not have enough resources, and lack honest personnel. Unfortunately, some of these anti-corruption commissions still have to report to the president of the country or the corrupt legislative. This goes a long way in reducing the effectiveness of the organization and makes them more subjected to politicking. In some countries, these institutions do not have enough power to impose penalties and their reports may not be eventually followed up by any other institution.

8.   Transparency of law/code of conducts

When what the law dictates is not entirely clear or open to several interpretations, it opens up the ground for corruption. What does this mean? Rules can get confusing, especially when the documents are not available to the public. In some cases, laws are amended without public knowledge. Other times, laws are written in languages that are not clear to the populace but only to trained lawyers, thereby leaving room for different interpretations.

Sometimes the procedure for public projects is also not clear and so it may be difficult to fully understand the process that was followed before a decision was reached.

9. Examples set by leaders

The pattern displayed by leadership is another contributing factor to the development of corruption. When leadership does not provide the right examples either through their engagement in acts of corruption or through the turning of a blind eye to corrupt practices especially by friends, families, political party members, etc., citizens and public-sector employees cannot be expected to be incorruptible. The same also extends to public intuitions such as tax agency, the police, customs, etc. *"A rotten head cannot produce a healthy body."*

10. Inefficiency of public bureaucracy

From country to country, the quality of bureaucracy varies. In some countries, a job in the public sector comes with prestige and a good standard of living while in many others, the reverse is the case. When citizens perceive that there is less corruption in the public sector and recruitments and promotions are based on merits rather than nepotism, they tend to engage in corrupt acts themselves. The quality of bureaucracy is improved by the absence of politically-motivating hiring, nepotism, and patronage. Proper incentives and a real tradition of transparency go a long way in quenching the interest of the interests in corrupt practices.

Chapter Four

Manifestation of Corruption
The FIFA Scandal—A Case Study on Bribery

The first of these case studies will be the 2015 FIFA Bribery Scandal which vibrated across several nations and caused wounds in the hearts of many soccer fans all around the world.

Public arrests

The United States Federal prosecutors issued cases of corruption amongst officials linked to the international football, futsal, and beach soccer governing body, FIFA in 2015. By the end of May, fourteen people have been indicted on wire fraud, racketeering, and money laundering charges in an investigation carried out by the FBI and the Internal Revenue Service-Criminal Investigation Division (IRS-CI).

Initially, seven FIFA officials were arrested at a hotel in Switzerland where the 65th FIFA Congress and the election of the new president of FIFA were scheduled to be held. The officials were arrested on allegations of receiving $150 million in bribes. Before the arrest, former

CONCACAF president Jack Warner and Alejandro Burzaco, a marketing executive surrendered themselves to the police. The hotel raid later went on to trigger a series of arrests in Australia, Colombia, Germany, Costa Rica, and Switzerland with numerous criminal investigation cases opened against FIFA on the grounds of corruption.

The string of arrests were made on the allegations of the use of bribery, fraud, and money laundering to illegally issue media and marketing rights for the FIFA games in North and South America to the tune of $150 million, with one-third of this sum connected to the Copa America Centenario, which was to be hosted in the US.

In addition to this, there were further allegations that bribery was involved in the awards of sponsorship contracts, the selection process for the South Africa 2010 FIFA World Cup, the 2011 FIFA presidential election, and the bid for the 2022 FIFA World Cup. Multiple sources have also named NIKE in the corruption scandal with the allegation that the sports equipment company paid over $40 million in bribes to become the only provider of jerseys, footwear, sporting accessories, and equipment for the national team of Brazil.

How it all started

In late 2010, the FBI began investigating a CONCACAF official Chuck Blazer in a separate organized crime unrelated to the FIFA scandal. In August 2011, the IRS-CI also began their investigation into Blazer's failure to pay personal income tax. Toward the end of that year, the IRS-CI got wind of FBI's investigation on Blazer, and both decided to collaborate in the inquiry of the soccer executive. They decided to investigate the involvement of Blazer in the selection process for the hosting of the FIFA World Cup for the past three decades. At this point, it is instructive to note that the US taxes the net income of its citizens irrespective of where the source is, anywhere in the world. The US also makes it mandatory that taxpayers report and pay any tax on illegal income. The country also exercises universal jurisdiction over any financial institution with account holders based in the US.

Blazer eventually pled guilty to 10 criminal charges that include wire fraud conspiracy, money laundering, and other offenses related to income tax and banking. Blazer pleaded guilty to these charges to avoid facing a weightier charge of racketeering which comes with a prison sentence of 20 years.

On May 27, 2015, the charging document used in place of an indictment for a plea bargain was revealed. On the same day, seven other FIFA officials were arrested in their hotel rooms in Zurich, Switzerland. Blazer had made a secret recording of his meetings with FIFA officials and at one time concealed a recording device in a key ring during the London 2012 Olympics.

What the law says

The United States Department of Justice has not indicted any FIFA executive on the charge of bribery since federal bribery laws pertain to government officials only. Instead, what the prosecutors do is present charges of racketeering, wire fraud, and money laundering as permitted under the Racketeer Influenced and Corrupt Organizations Act, RICO. FIFA officials were also charged with violating the Travel Act. The act criminalizes the use of mail or any facility in interstate commerce for the promotion, management, or establishment of illegal activity. Bribery is an activity that is considered illegal under this act and is prosecutable under state and federal laws.

Extensions of the case

The corruption case didn't just stop in Europe and the Americas, it also extended to Africa.

There were allegations that in 2008, FIFA's general secretary, Jerome Valcke transferred $10 million; money that had been given to FIFA by the president of the South African Football Association, Danny Jordan, to an account said to be in control of Jack Warner, the head of CONCACAF as at the time. This payment was an important part of the US's indictment of Warner for receiving a bribe in exchange for helping South Africa secure the rights to host the 2010 FIFA World Cup. The payment made by Danny Jordan on behalf of the South African Football Association was intended for the development of football in South America and the Caribbean. But investigations revealed that Warner used $1.6 million to pay for personal loans and credit cards while over $300,000 was withdrawn by people close to him as a supermarket chain, JTA Supermarkets also benefited from the cash payment to the tune of $4.86 million.

Still on Africa, in May 2011, there was a publication in The Sunday Times against Issa Hayatou, the president of CAF about how he along with another Executive Committee member, Jacques Anouma received $1, 500,000 in bribes from Qatar to help the country receive hosting right for the 2022 FIFA World Cup.

In South America

Back to South America, in 2013, the former president of FIFA, Joao Haveange and the president of the Brazilian Football Confederation were both found guilty of receiving bribes to the tune of millions of dollars. Another FIFA executive committee member, Manilal Fernando was handed a lifetime ban for bribery and corruption. As at the end of 2016, eighteen individuals and two organizations have been indicted for various corruption charges. This includes nine FIFA officials and five businessmen.

1. Bribery

Bribery can be defined as the unethical use of gifts and favors for the achievement of personal aims. Bribery can either be initiated by someone who seeks or solicits bribes or a person who offers and then go ahead to pay them. Bribery is probably the most common manifestation of corruption, and its definition or definitions appear in the international laws of many countries as well as different academic and legal publications.

Worldwide, there are numerous complaints about politicians and political office holders who receive bribes and enrich their own pockets at a huge cost to the typical citizen.

In many countries, collecting and giving bribes is a crime punishable by as much as five years in jail. In a country like China, government officials found guilty of bribery often face punishments like life imprisonment or execution. Bribery is the most common manifestation of corruption. Money, material gifts, sex, company shares, employment, and even political office positions are usually given as bribes while the gain can be anything from preferential treatment, subversion of due process, and have a crime or error in judgment overlooked.

People who complain about other people using their positions of power to receive bribes are often quick to forget that those who give bribes are as corrupt as those who pay them and should, therefore, receive an equal measure of punishment. This is evident in the way some people think that presenting a "gift" to a public official or someone in a position of power to curry favor isn't wrong, but it's just a way of "being easily remembered."

For anyone serious about fighting corruption, steps have to be taken to prevent politicians and public officials from accepting gifts or any other form of gratification.

In many countries around the world, the acceptance of bribery is publicly denounced. The congressman is publicly vilified for using his political influence and legislative power to endorse proposals or affect the award of contracts to his cronies. However, in private, the beneficiaries of his power justify his actions as the right approach. For such people, they see the congressman as a pragmatic person and one that is "current with the times."

In many developing countries, many think that the payment of bribes ensures the smooth running of the society. Many have the mindset that without handing out a gift from time to time (especially during the Easter, Christmas, Diwali, Hanukkah, Eid, New Year period, during house-warming, child's birth, or marriage ceremony) to someone in a position of power whether in a government or private establishment, that they might lose an existing contract or open up a space that the competition can exploit. For them, this might be a great loss, because it means that a sales potential is lost. The mindset of these people is that the cost of a gift item is quite insignificant to the profit they will be able to make if they can "lock down" this influential person. Besides, many of these people often factor in the cost of bribing such official(s) which they then add to the total cost of the contract they are trying to get. As a result of this, goods and services cost way more than they are ordinarily supposed to cost since these goods have already been budgeted for.

If corruption is looked at from an economic perspective, then on the macroeconomic scale, it comes at a huge financial loss to the society. Also, at that microeconomic level, bribing is a profitable option for the entrepreneur. When an entrepreneur pays a bribe to secure a contract, which on normal grounds should have been given to someone else, it causes harm to other entrepreneurs, the national economy, and the world economy. This is because the decision to subvert due process is not the best of decisions since the right candidate or the best producer does not win. It means the best product is not manufactured. Even though the payment for the contracts still ends up in the economy, but because the bribe-payer has budgeted the cost of bribing officials into his cost of production, a burden is hung on the necks of consumers or taxpayers from a purely macroeconomic point of view.

For example, in Kenya, the results of the investigation have shown that a Kenyan spends a little over 100 Euros a month on the payment of bribes to officials, which is about a third of his average monthly income. Typically, reports have it that a Kenyan will probably have to "settle" his way out of situations more than ten times every month and more than half of those hours, a police officer is involved in the settlement. A condition which makes Kenyan businesses earmark around 3 percent of their average turnover for the sole aim of bribing a government official or another agency.

There are different specific types of bribery, and they include the following:

- Influence-peddling: In this kind of bribery, public officials use their political or public office to exert influence that is ordinarily not available to outsiders. This is quite different from legitimate political advocacy commonly known as "lobbying" because in this case, the corrupt public official is selling the access he/she has in influencing the decision-making process of the government. Access that he/she has, only as a result of holding that public office.

- Offer and receipt of improper gift: This is a very delicate scenario as it is one that involves the definition of what is improper. What is considered as an improper gift varies from country to country, and culture to culture. In some countries, the culture doesn't frown on public officials receiving tips or gratuities for the discharge of their duties. In cases like these, even if the payment is not linked to the interest of any applicant, it becomes difficult to distinguish such forms of bribery or extortion since there will always be a connection between payments and results.

- Bribing to avoid being liable for the payment of tax and other civic duties: Public officials who work for government revenue agencies such as customs officers and IRS agents may be bribed in exchange for reduced tax payment or overall elimination of the taxes to be collected by the government.

  This bribery can also extend to turning a blind eye to evidence of wrongdoing such as trafficking and smuggling, money laundering, and tax infractions.

- Bribing to provide a backing for fraud: Government payroll officials may be bribed to participate in payroll frauds, such as payment for fictitious or non-existent workers such also known as ghost workers.

- Bribing to avoid criminal prosecution: Officers of the law, judges, and prosecutors may be bribed by corrupt citizens to ensure that their activities are not investigated or if prosecuted, ensure that they receive a favorable judgment in the court of law.

- Bribing to get an undue advantage over a resource or resources: Public and even private-sector officials may be bribed to ensure that the party greasing the palm gets the contracts and on terms favorable. It is not unusual to find that contracts are purposely unlawfully inflated to account for this bribe. In a case when this is not done, part of the proceeds of the bribe are usually used to pay the official as a kickback or hidden commission.

- Private-sector bribery: This form of bribery often occurs in banking and financial institutions with the award of loans which do not meet the minimum criteria for security and which often do not get paid back. In many of these cases, the financial cost of damage done in the long run often exceeds the sum collected for the bribe.

- Bribery in exchange for confidential information: Top officials who are privy to top secret information are often the targets of bribery which aim to entice them into disclosing these secrets in exchange for monetary benefits or other forms of benefits. Cases like this happen in both public and private sectors, and are known as espionage. It also extends to such things as using secret information to trade stocks or securities unfairly. This is known as insider trading.

2.   Embezzlement and Fraud

When someone embezzles money, they use the access that their positions offer to illegally use the money for their gain. In the case of fraud, it is the use of deception to make people part with their monies. Within the boundaries of the discussion of corruption, embezzlement, fraud, and theft all involve the receipt of money or the conversion of property or other valuable things without being legally entitled to them, but has obtained them by position and employment.

3.   Blackmail & Extortion

While bribery involves the persuasion of others for the achievement of corrupt aims, extortion involves the use of threats whether physical or psychological to coerce a victim into giving up their money or do something they wouldn't otherwise do. Police can blackmail crime suspects with false imprisonment. An individual can be threatened with the release of their private information as well as violence if they fail to carry out an action or part with sums of money. It is not rare for influential people to threaten to go to social media or report to higher authorities, if they do not receive the service they demand even at the expense of other people. In many situations also, an official who has committed acts of corruption may be threatened with exposure. In many countries, it is also not unusual to find that civil servants demand payment for "express service" to ensure that consideration and decision-making process is expedited.

4.   Abuse of discretion

Corruption also manifests itself in the abuse of discretionary power for personal gains without any coercion or inducement from foreign elements. For example, a top official of a government or private firm may abuse his discretionary authority by deciding to make his department purchase goods and services from a company in which he or she holds an interest. This kind of abuse of power and discretion is often widespread in organizations where there is extensive bureaucracy with little oversight and accountability structures as well as those organizations where the decision-making process is so complicated that it makes the decision process itself ineffective.

5.   Favoritism & Nepotism

These cases also feature the characteristics of a situation where discretion is abused. The only difference is that in the event of favoritism and nepotism, the choice is not motivated by self-interest but instead that of the preference of an individual close to the corrupt person either by blood, membership of the same political party, religious organization, ideological group, etc. For instance, if an official hires a relative over another applicant to advance his family's interest and not on merit, then he is corrupt. Nepotism also shows its face in the favoring of (or discrimination against) individuals based on race, disability, religious affiliations, sexual orientation, or membership and club associations.

6. Conduct which creates or exploits conflicting interests

According to the United Nations Manual on Anti-Corruption Policy, most forms of corruption either involve the creation or the exploitation of conflict between what is considered to be the professional duties of an individual and his/her interests. When a bribe is paid, the operation of that conflict increases since many cases of embezzlement happen because a person was unable to control his/her temptation, but instead yield to it by taking undue advantage of the conflict that has already been in place. What is this conflict of interest? In any business, whether private or public sector, employees and officials are always confronted with situations that make it difficult to choose between those decisions which are in their best interest and those that are going to be of benefits to their employees.

7. Unethical political contributions

One of the most difficult anti-corruption measures is being able to identify which donations made to a political party or organization are legitimate and not meant to unduly influence the present or future activities of such members of a party when they become elected to office. It is not illegal or seen as a corrupt act to make donations to support a party to increase their chance of being elected. In fact, in some countries, donations to support a political party are a vital part of the political system and as such are guarded by the Constitution. But if a gift is made with the intention of influencing a party's or candidate's decisions in such a way that it favors the donor over the interest of the public, then that is a fraudulent act; there is no link between the payment and any particular action on the recipient. Political donations are quite hard to regulate since donations can come in various forms such as cash payments, low-interest loans, the gift of goods and services, or even in intangible forms such as favors in the interest of the party. One can measure that what will work in preventing corruption involving political donations is to limit the size of contributions to prevent one single donor from having a dominant influence.

Another approach is to take measures that ensure transparency through the full disclosure of anything donated so that both the donor and recipient are politically accountable.

Chapter Five

Cost of Corruption to the Society

The impact of corruption is multi-dimensional as it has political, economic, social, and environmental ramifications. Politically, corruption presents a blockade to the rule of law, especially in a democratic system of government.

In a democratic regime of government, corruption makes public institutions lose their transparency and legitimacy which is often manifested in the misuse of power for private gains. And, this is very harmful to democracy, particularly newly emerging ones. It is almost impossible to develop a leadership structure that has accountability at its core when the climate is corrupt.

Widespread corruption may also result in the rise of negative consequences such as cynicism, voters' apathy and reduction of interest in political participation resulting in political instability. Corruption can also lead to a decrease in transparency of political decision making, distortion of political development, and unfair silencing of political competition such as assassination and kidnap.

Socially, corruption sows the seed of discord amongst people, and they won't want to work together for the common interest. Since corruption brings apathy with it, the society becomes weak at taking decisive and bold steps. Payment of bribes becomes the norm. The social strata become wider as the middle class disappears gradually due to the widening gap between the wealthy and the have-nots. Social vices increase as jealousy, hatred, and insecurity become the order of the day. A quick look at African leadership in the past shows that the corruption many African leaders advance is what eventually led to their downfall. Through the undermining of the legitimacy of government, reduction of productivity, hindrances to development, worsening of poverty, oppression of the poor, instigation of civil unrest and many more infractions led to their eventual downfalls. In the worst case scenario, corruption may result in loss of life. Second to this is the loss of freedom, health, or money.

Professionally, in a corrupt system, quality of service will lack since mediocrity will be the order of the day. So, anyone who demands quality will have to pay a very high price to get it.

Widespread corruption often leads to a general disregard and disdain for public officials even when a particular public official has not been accused of any wrongdoing. Disregard, in turn, brings along with it distrust which can lead to a state of civil unrest. Respect is very crucial in rulership. It is a critical criterion in the maintenance of a stable social life. People often vote for leaders they respect besides the belief that this person is going to help improve their living conditions. People do not like to vote for candidates who they think are corrupt. During the 2016 presidential election, one of the rhetoric that President Trump used to his advantage is the constant labeling of Hilary Clinton as a corrupt politician who shouldn't be trusted.

In one of his numerous rallies, Trump said, *"...we are also going to end government corruption. Hillary Clinton is the most corrupt person ever to run for President...Clinton and her cronies have sacrificed your security, your family's safety, and your country's safety as though it meant nothing at all. Remember, also, that Hillary lied under oath to Congress saying she had never sent or received classified information on her insecure server, and pretended not to know that the letter "C" meant confidential information that was classified. Hillary then told the FBI she couldn't remember 39 times, and then, in written testimony last week under oath, said she couldn't remember another 21 times. This is elaborate criminal cover-up included Hillary's deleting and bleaching of 33,000 emails, the disappearance of 13 phones, two boxes of email evidence gone missing, and the destruction of laptops in a secret deal with the FBI. This is many times worse than Watergate. And we're going to put an end to it on November 8th. Another series of leaked emails show top officials in the Clinton campaign scheming to take massive sums of money from registered foreign lobbyists. But you don't hear the media talking about it..."*

This strategy of hanging Clinton on a stake of corruption worked for Donald Trump since he has not previously held any public office and appeared to the Americans populace as "one of them." Even when the Clinton camp launched a reprisal by attacking Trump's patriotism (since he never made public his tax returns and had repeatedly made it known that he has no intention of doing so) it was a weak strategy since Trump had extensively leveraged on Clinton's antecedents as a former US Senator and Secretary of State to show that politicians are not to be trusted.

Corruption also has both major and minor effects economically. Either way, they both negatively impact the individual and the society by extension. The first of this is the fact that corruption causes the national wealth of a country to deplete.

Corruption is often a primary culprit for the increase in prices of goods and services, particularly in developing countries. The use of scarce public assets to fund, "white elephant" projects at the expense of much needed and necessary projects such as schools, hospitals & roads, portable water supply is also another effect of corruption on the society.

In many developing countries of Africa where corruption is ravaging through, funds are always diverted and misappropriated, public assets are personalized, inflation rate soars, economic development is not balanced, good work ethics and professionalism is found wanting, unhealthy competition arises, and poverty level rises within the population.

Economically, corruption causes a distortion in the market and the allocation of resources for the following reasons:

• It reduces the government's ability to enforce necessary regulatory controls and inspections to correct for market failures. When the government is unable to perform its regulatory functions on banks, manufacturing industries, transportation, financial markets, and hospitals, it loses its essential functions. On the other hand, when government's intervention in these areas is inspired by corruption, monopolies for private benefits can be created;

• Incentives are distorted since individuals instead of channeling their efforts to productive activities divert that to the rent seeking;

• It leads to excessive and unjustified costs. Corruption causes high welfare costs; the cost of negotiating and paying a bribe and the cost of looking for someone who is susceptible to the receipt of the bribe all adds up. When there is corruption, contractual obligations are not kept, and costs pile up;

• It reduces and blurs the core role of the government such as the enforcement of laws, protection of the rights of citizens and their businesses, etc. When the rights to a fair hearing is trampled upon, when contractual obligations are not adhered to, when citizens are not allowed to demonstrate their rights because of corruption, economic growth may be stunted,

• It makes less legitimate the market economy and even democracy. In fact, in many countries transiting to a democracy where there are widespread criticisms against democracy and the market economy, corruption has often been the most motivating factor for these criticisms.

• It increases poverty since the income earning power of the poor is reduced.

For all of these reasons, corruption slows down economic growth.

In countries such as Ukraine, Russia, and Indonesia, small businesses are often pressured by public officials to make payments to make something happen or prevent something from happening. In Indonesia, for example, these payments are often known as "pungli" and can account for as much as 20 percent of the operating costs of business—the equivalent of the imposition of high tax sales. In Nigeria, the locals call these payments "egunje." The kind of corruption that increases the cost of doing business affects small businesses the most as they are coerced and bullied by bureaucrats into making payments that the government does not recognize. The cost in time that the owners of businesses must spend to comply with these demands also add to the unnecessary requirements imposed on them.

In many countries around the world, the small businesses drive the economy, which means that when they do not grow, the growth of the economy slows, unemployment increases and the rate of poverty soars. This is often the case in developing countries and even more for economies that are in transition.

Large businesses can more easily protect themselves from these overbearing public officials because they have departments whose specialization is to handle these bureaucrats. They are also able to engage the services of individuals who are adept at handling opaque regulations and tax laws. Their sheer size also makes them resistant to petty extortion. They are also influential and can use their powers to protect themselves from extortion or get more contracts that can balance out the charges being a demand by aggressive bureaucrats. For example, it is not uncommon for large organizations to veil bribes in the form of gifts or donations to acquire larger market shares through the weakening of competition, tax cuts, or other benefits.

Chapter Six

Measuring Corruption

How possible is it to know the level of corruption in a system? You can't reduce what you can't measure nor fight what you don't see. The nature of corruption makes it difficult to measure since people go to great lengths to hide corrupt practices. Again, since corruption manifests itself in various ways, it is quite difficult to measure it. Looking at the number of bribes paid or received by a government institution for the award of a contract as a measurement of corruption will neglect other acts of corruption such as favoritism and nepotism in hiring. If one then attempts to measure fraudulent acts instead of the amount paid for bribes, then one would end have to deal with a lot of relatively unimportant actions and then determine whether truly each one is a corrupt act. Still, one would not have the information. Even though there is no direct way to measure the level of corruption, one can still get information about its prevalence rate in any country or organization.

Relevant information can be sourced from:

1. Corruption reports as published in reputable newspapers. Examples include: The New York Times, The Washington Post, The Economist, and Le Monde. The internet today has also become an excellent source of breaking valuable information regarding corruption.

2. Case studies of organizations or countries based on corruption. The problem with this option is that such reports are not usually made public.

3. Surveys. The use of surveys is also a good choice. The use of questionnaire-based survey doesn't actually measure corruption but perceptions of corruption. Many international agencies use these reviews a lot in the planning of their programs. For instance, The World Bank has used these surveys extensively in Tanzania, India, and many other countries especially in the area of healthcare development. Studies can be obtained from Global Competitiveness Report, Transparency International, and Political Risk Services.

The reports published by these bodies are being used extensively by researchers. For instance, one of the most widely used is Transparency International index which rates corrupt nations on a scale of 0 to 100.

In 2016, Transparency International published its Corruption Perception Index.

Out of the 176 countries where the surveys were carried out, these are the Top 10 Most Corrupt Countries.

1. Somalia

    Region: Sub-Saharan Africa

    Score: 10

2. South Sudan

    Region: Sub-Saharan Africa

    Score: 11

3. North Korea

    Region: Asia Pacific

    Score: 12

4. Syria

    Region: The Middle East and North Africa

    Score: 13

5. Yemen

    Region: The Middle East and North Africa

    Score: 14

6. Sudan

Region: The Middle East and North Africa

Score: 14

7. Libya

Region: The Middle East and North Africa

Score: 14

8. Afghanistan

Region: Asia Pacific

Score: 15

9. Guinea-Bissau

Region: Sub-Saharan Africa

Score: 16

10. Venezuela

Region: Americas

Score: 17

In the analysis of the survey, Transparency International explains that *"Over two-thirds of the 176 countries and territories in this year's index fall below the midpoint of our scale of 0 (highly corrupt) to 100 (very clean). The global average score is a paltry 43, indicating endemic corruption in a country's public sector. Top-scoring countries are far outnumbered by countries where citizens face the tangible impact of corruption on a daily basis. This year's results highlight...a vicious circle between corruption, unequal distribution of power in society, and unequal distribution of wealth."*

On the other hand, this is a list of Top Ten Least Corrupt Countries:

1. Denmark

    Region: Europe and Central Asia

    Score: 90

2. New Zealand

    Region: Asia Pacific

    Score: 90

3. Finland

    Region: Europe and Central Asia

    Score: 89

4. Sweden

    Region: Europe and Central Asia

    Score: 88

5. Switzerland

    Region: Europe and Central Asia

    Score: 86

6. Norway

    Region: Europe and Central Asia

    Score: 85

7. Singapore

    Region: Europe and Central Asia

    Score: 84

8. Netherlands

    Region: Europe and Central Asia

    Score: 83

9. Canada

    Region: Americas

    Score: 82

10. Germany

    Region: Europe and Central Asia

    Score: 81

A breakdown of the study by region showed that corruption ricocheted in every part of the world.

In the Americas: The Panama Papers leaked in April 2016, the FIFA scandal and the $3.5 billion US dollars Odebrecht settlement in Brazil in the last month of the year put the continent on the corruption spotlight for the year.

In Sub-Sahara Africa: 2016 was the year of elections for a few African countries including the United States. In Ghana, for instance, there were mentions of rigging at the polls with the president breaking the internet for plagiarizing the speech of a former US president. It is important also to note that the 2016 election for the first time, an incumbent president will be voted out. But that's not all for the continent, in The Gambia, a country of fewer than 9 million people, for the first time, the people also voted out Yahya Jammeh who has held on to power for 22 years.

Yaya in the wake of the announcement congratulated Adama Barrow, his successor, only some days later to go back on his decision to hand over power by citing irregularities in the election as a reason for not accepting defeat. It took a show of force by the Nigerian and Senegalese Military and persuasion by the president of Mauritania to get him to step down. Yahya Jammeh has been alleged to steal over $10 million dollars of public funds amongst other allegations.

The Middle East and North Africa: Terrorism and Arab spring have led to political instability in the region in the past six years. The area did not experience any growth in the fight against corruption and impunity. In the index, more than 90% of countries have scores below 50, which translates to a failing grade.

In Asia and the Pacific: Countries like North Korea and Indonesia rank high on the corruption index. In China, despite the fact that corruption carries a death penalty, the rate hasn't significantly slowed down (China's president, Xi Jinping has been named in The Panama Papers). The region performed poorly because of lack of accountability on the part of government, insecurity, and intolerance for civil liberty.

Europe and Central Asia: The developed countries of Europe performed much better than other regions save for a few countries. However, this doesn't mean that the region is free from corruption.

Chapter Seven

Reducing Corruption—The Role of the Government

Earlier, we have discussed the many factors that contribute to the growth of corruption in a country. It is worthy to note that some of these factors abound more in poor and developing countries and transition economies.

However, at some point, economic development tends to bring about a reduction in corruption. That notwithstanding, even at the same level of economic development, some countries are higher in corruption perception index than their counterparts.

Some countries such as Singapore and Hong Kong lately have stepped up the fight against corruption and have achieved good results. Governments have an active role in the reduction of corruption in the society. With well-coordinated strategy and efforts, corruption can be reduced to the bare minimum even though complete eradication is not achievable. Trying to do so will only waste resources without the achievement of the objective. For instance, trying to eradicate corruption might lead to harsh penalties that will violate several civil rights, costly structural or organizational or legal changes, and very high public sector wages to mention a few. Therefore, it is more realistic to think about bringing corruption to the barest minimum than try to completely eradicate it.

Since the causes of corruption are multifactorial, the solution to it is not that simple. Some factors can be quickly eliminated while others may not be so easily done or even impossible to eradicate. Because corruption is involved, the war against it must be waged from different angles using combinations of different strategies. It is a war that will take time. It may not be won in months or even five or ten years. It will not be won by the reliance on a single strategy or the exertion of excessive action in a single solution such as setting up an anti-corruption commission, increasing salaries of public workers, or formulating stiffer penalties.

Any strategy that must be employed must take into account the fact that there are people who demand corrupt acts and there are those who accept/condone acts of corruption, whether in the private or public sector. This means that for corruption to thrive, there must exist a demand and supply of it.

Factors that affect the application for corruption include:

1. Governmental regulations and authorizations

2. Certain features of taxation

3. Some spending decisions

4. The supply of goods below prevailing market prices

A few examples of factors that affect the amount of corruption include:

1. Bureaucracy in the public system

2. Wages in the public sector

3. Mismatch of crimes and penalties

4. Controls by institutions

5. Transparency within the government, judiciary, electoral processes, etc.

6. Examples laid by leaders

And just like in the core economics of demand and supply, price affects both. Different incentives play a role in determining how elastic or inelastic these requirements or supplies are. In the simplest scenario of corruption, the bribery needs something (a benefit above others or reduction in cost) from an official and is willing to bribe to get it. The official in question also has something to sell (influence over a decision or process) and wants to be rewarded for sticking his neck out and applying efforts.

However, the state is in all of this as all these actions are being carried out in the framework the state has constructed. The state to an appreciable extent is responsible for creating the environment that allows these activities to thrive through its policies and actions (or inactions).

In an ideal world, the public official is an honest and faithful channel through which the citizen interacts with the state. The public official executes the mandate of the state as directed. But we do not live in an ideal world partly because of the opaque policies of the state, partly because of the nature of bureaucracies, and partly because of human nature.

Sometimes, instructions on the execution of policies are not communicated because even the policy makers do not have a clear idea of what they are doing or they have just decided to be opaque in their actions. Complete transparency may often imply less power since their discretionary ability is significantly reduced when everything is clear to all concerned. The point is that the war against corruption is not different and separate from strategies involved in state reformation. The same measures and strategy involved in fighting corruption are also those needed to reform the state.

The war on "black money" by India's Prime Minister, Narendra Modi is a prime example of anti-corruption measures that are also rebuilding the state. In India, black money or cash unaccounted-for is a huge problem for the country because it keeps cash out of the reach of the banks making it unavailable for lending to business, thus, hindering the growth of business and causing economic stagnation. Black money also causes the taxes collected by the government to reduce hence hindering it from performing its obligations to the citizens.

In India, about one-third of business transactions are conducted with black money. Businesspeople give bribe to government officials in exchange for operating licenses and other forms of approvals. The staff take these funds and then invest them in real estate while understating the amount they are paid. So, what happens is that the government officials do not only buy land and other properties with cash that is unaccounted for, but the sellers also pay the lesser tax than they are supposed to because the price of these properties has been understated. Everyday transactions such as payments to beauticians are also not recorded so that they do not have to pay the tax on these sales.

In a very bold and audacious move, the prime minister has decided to ban the two largest bills of one of the most populous countries in the world with over 1 billion people. 500 rupees—an equivalent of $7.50—and 1000 rupees account for over 80 percent of the currency in circulation in India. A country where more than 70 percent of transactions are carried out in cash. Under this plan, Indians are expected to exchange old bills for new one of 500 and 2,000 rupees. But this can only be done at banks and post offices where the exchange process can be monitored by officials and anyone with the unusually large amount of cash will have to explain its source to authorities. Expectedly, the change has been met with both positive and negative reactions. A very good idea with bad execution!

The idea behind the plan was to expose and penalize those corrupt people who have large amounts of cash they cannot account for, primarily cash on which taxes have not been remitted. Most of this black money is held in the 500 and 1000 rupees note—which is now banned. What this means is that anyone who wants to exchange cash that is more than 250,000 rupees in cash (3,700) must have tenable reasons for being in possession of that huge sum when the tax authorities come calling. If the reasons are genuine enough and the evidence of paid taxes are tendered, then the person is allowed to keep it. Otherwise, these individuals will be subjected to further questioning and possible prosecution by the authorities.

While many consider it disruptive, others consider this plan a necessary evil in the fight against corruption. Sometimes, things have to be difficult before they can get better. Many people found that there wasn't enough cash to perform simple transactions such as buying food, fuel, and paying for transportation.

To avoid alerting people who are evading taxes, the Prime Minister ordered that the new bills should not be printed until after the announcement has been made neither did it make the new bills available for dispensation by ATMs.

Now the question many are asking is: will people not just go ahead and hoard the new bills? The result explained earlier that reducing corruption requires a combination of strategies as an excessive effort in a single strategy often doesn't work. The prime minister must, first of all, find a way to enforce stiff penalties on citizens that are avoiding tax to make tax avoidance unattractive to people. If people see keeping their money in banks as the right thing to do, cash will be more available for lending and people will form a habit of paying taxes.

Because a very high percentage of Indians are unbanked, the government could not dispense altogether with cash. If citizens continued to hoard these new notes, India might find itself in this same problem. Therefore, the way forward will be to combine the currency ban with an aggressive stance on endemic bribery that is driving India's public system.

Still on fighting corruption, many believe that the relative wages of public officials are an important variable in the level of corruption in a country. For example, in Singapore, a country with an excellent corruption perception index and where the level of corruption has reduced so much in recent years, its public officials receive some of the highest wages in the world. It is also noteworthy that the civil service of Singapore is small in size, commands respects, and enjoys a high status.

In countries where the wages in the public sector are very low, especially when compared to what obtains in the private sector. This usually happens due to public policies that have inflated the number of people in the civil service. In other words, the state has sacrificed wages for a high number of public servants. The great number of employees results in low wages. In this kind of scenario, it will be unwise to advise that such countries simply increase their salaries without actually shedding the size of their civil service. But dropping the size of the public service might be devastating, at least politically, especially if having a defined number of civil servants is an objective for the government and if the government believes that public sector hiring is a panacea to unemployment.

Another way to fight corruption is to have solid regulations in place. Sometimes, quasi-fiscal regulations can be a substitute for taxing and spending actions. For example, countries with the lowest corruption perception index: Sweden, Denmark, Canada, etc. have some of the highest tax burdens. While on the other hand, some of the countries perceived to be highly corrupt: Pakistan, Bangladesh, Indonesia, Venezuela, etc. have very low tax burdens. In these countries, quasi-fiscal regulations are used in place of taxes and public expenditures. This means that countries that are serious about eliminating corruption would have to replace quasi-fiscal regulations with properly structured taxing and public spending.

As an extension of the above, tax incentives should not be left to the discretion of public officials; doing so gives enough room for corruption to develop. An easy way to stop corruption through taxation will be to remove tax incentives and instead create tax systems with lower rates and broad bases. Even though there is a distinct advantage in this, unfortunately, many governments use tax incentives to lure foreign investors.

These governments also try to provide goods and services at prices below the prevailing market price. Such goods and services include public housing, fuel, education, utility services, etc. But often, public officials exploit the subsidy strategy. Subsidy creates excess demand and the need to ration the service or goods. Rationing encourages corruption. Therefore, it makes sense that government tries to raise prices to very close or at par with the prevailing market price in a bid to eliminate corruption.

Chapter Nine

Corruption and the media

The role of the media in any society cannot be overemphasized irrespective of the system of government that such an organization practices. In a democratic regime of government, as practiced in many countries today, the media is often seen as the fourth pillar that the system relies on. The press is tasked with the responsibility of monitoring, investigating, and reporting on the actions of those directing the affairs of government. Despite this, the media itself is not incorruptible as many cases around the world have shown.

While many people do not perceive the media and journalists as corrupt especially as compared to politicians and public officials, many still generally agree that the press needs to be legally-protected, accountable to the people, and held to the highest standard of professionalism and ethics.

Factors affecting corruption in the Media

In many developing countries of the world, the media faces the problem of low remuneration, inadequate training and proper technical skills, low professional standards—all of which creates a breeding ground for corruption. In well-developed countries, the issue of ownership creates an opportunity for the media to be compromised as it is sometimes the case that government owns and controls some media houses while the ones that are owned by private individuals usually fall victim to political manipulation and legal frameworks that are not democratic.

Legal framework

- **Freedom of speech**

The legal framework of a country plays a direct role in the integrity of the journalists and their ability to resist unnecessary influence and make public issues of partiality. This is usually the case in many developing countries where the tenets of democracy are not firmly established. In such a system, the media may be hindered from performing its job as a whistleblower by systemic restrictions imposed on it.

Freedom of speech and expression is an essential prerequisite for unbiased reporting and coverage, and it is from this that press freedom and freedom of media are gotten. This right is enshrined in article 19 of the Universal Declaration of Human Rights (UDHR) and also in section 19 of the UN Covenant on Civil and Political Rights and is considered as critical tools in the fight for the right to freedom of expression. Despite this, many UN countries still do not adhere to this agreement regardless of the fact that they are legally bound to it.

In some developing countries, freedom of expression can be limited through censorship by government for instance-the Chinese government's blocking of websites, regulatory systems bordering on oppression as seen in Saudi Arabia and Belarus, state domination of the media as seen in North Korea and Cuba, and the victimization and imprisonment of journalists as seen in Eritrea, Syria, and Uzbekistan. For instance, up until 2012 in Myanmar, journalists were subjected to direct censorship by the state and had to turn in their reports to state censors before they were disseminated to the public.

In some countries, a specific part of the legal framework directly limits media coverage and consequently affects freedom of expression. In Jordan for instance, the penal code prescribes imprisonments for journalists who provide coverage on issues that 'could breach national unity, divide the population or damage the image and the reputation of the state.' In Saudi Arabia ISPs (Internet Service Providers) are mandated to keep watch over users of their services who visits forbidden websites. In some other countries, the government officials are adequately protected by law against criticism in the media, which therefore makes it harder for journalists to beam searchlights on their actions.

Elsewhere, the law does not make provisions for the security of journalists. In these countries, while the freedom of speech and expression might be recognized and acknowledge, it is only so in principle and not in actual practice; since there are no provisions on a ground for the adequate protection of journalist in their duties and against attacks whether physical or in the form of defamation suits.

A particular example would be in Honduras where in principle the country acknowledges press freedom but puts in place laws that punish pressmen who provide coverage on pressing issues such as corruption in government, violation of human rights, drug trafficking, illegal dismissals, and even assassination of journalists.

A country may also use libel laws to stop the press from being free to report its activities. The report of A Media Foundation for West Africa shows that even though there has been a rise in media pluralism in the region in recent years but so has also been the case in the number of court cases involving the media. The author notes that such cases have at the center ruling government officials and top leaders of political parties. The report of another study shows that in African countries such as South Africa, Nigeria, Senegal, Ghana, Zambia, and Ethiopia, libel laws to protect the presidency are in place. In the case of Mali and Tanzania for instance, these laws extend to the parliaments too.

In the case of Zimbabwe, defamation law makes the work of journalists reporting on corruption harder. An example readily comes to mind: toward the end of 2010, the first lady of Zimbabwe, Grace Mugabe sued Standard newspaper over the publishing of Wikileaks report that Zimbabwe high ranking public officials including the first lady have been benefiting from diamond profits.

- **Right to Access Information**

The right to freedom of expression is also quite related to the right to access information. The right to access information makes it the obligation of government to ensure that the citizens and journalists get access to official government information. This provides that journalists can gather and dispense information in an unbiased manner. In many developing countries, there are often inadequate legal provisions for this. For instance, the report of a study conducted in 2010 shows that less than 7.5 % of African countries have an enforceable law that provides for the right to access information— very dark figure.

While there is no denying the fact that worldwide, there has been a growth in the number of countries that have made provisions for access to information, there is quite a lot who still refuse citizens and journalists access to public files due to a persistent culture of secrecy, little public awareness, insufficient capacity as well as institutional barriers.

- **Media Licensing and Registration**

This can be used as a tool by the government to muffle

the media. In Malaysia for instance, newspaper operators every year have to renew their licenses. The editors or workers who have been critical of government actions are victimized and often forced to resign. (Djankov et al. 2001). The payment of registration fees as a prerequisite to the registration of newspaper has been ruled by The African Commission on Human and People's Right as a restriction on press freedom.

Registration and licensing of journalists is another way the state controls the media. This is a widespread practice in both developing and developed countries. In a study of regulatory practices in over a hundred developing and developed countries, the result shows that for every four countries observed, government performs licensing role in at least one. In some other countries, the government will only give out press card to journalists who are trusted to abide by the government's instructions or guidelines.

In Saudi Arabia, the government has a right to the appointment and dismissal of the editor-in-chiefs of the country's newspapers. Such a power ensures that the government can direct the media as it so wishes.

- **Ownership**

The ownership of media houses plays a serious role in having a corruption-free press. Under ownership structure, there are four models available: state-ownership, private cooperation, public service broadcasting (PSB), and community media. In several instances, ownership of media is influenced by media regulation. State-owned media often have the widest reach in many developing countries, and of course, they tend to be biased toward the government in their reports.

A report by World Bank that looked into the ownership structure of media house in almost 100 countries shows that state-owned media are overall less efficient than their private counterparts. For instance, Kenya Broadcasting Corporation owned by the Kenyan government has the reach that extends beyond the urban area and well into rural areas. Its coverage also shows bias for the government. In Zimbabwe, the Zimbabwe Broadcasting Corporation owned by the government controls many TV and radio stations across the country and consistently provides coverage that is positively biased for the ruling party ZANU-PF.

Government-owned media also come under fire for bowing easily to political pressure and neglecting coverage of issues that undermine the administration. When the media is exclusively owned by private owners, it might also be restrained as seen in many Latin American countries.

In addition to this, transparency in ownership is also an issue as the owners behind many media companies are often not revealed to the public. This affects trust and integrity. Italy is an extreme example of a country where media control and political power lies in the hand of a single individual. In addition to all this, in many privately-owned media houses, journalists have to ensure that they are financially productive for the company in addition to their duty of informing the public about happenings. Many have to provide coverage for money and even sell news. If they are not able to meet funding target or are critical of funding agencies or organizations where the media outlet owners have interest, they may be fired.

- **Resources**

In a lot of developing countries, inadequate professional training, high staff turnover is responsible for the little professional standard of journalism. This makes the media much more likely to fall into the trap of corruption.

Small remuneration in a media where resources are scanty, it's likely to increase the susceptibility of journalists to corrupt practices. The fear of losing the job and salary cuts are seen as more important than ethics and thus makes it easy for journalists to compromise and comply with the dictates of superiors. Poor pay also often make African journalist abandon career to chase more financially rewarding options such as PR. In this case, they can get incentives in the form of a gift, cash, and entertainment which they can use to supplement their salaries. They can also get cash in exchange for favorable news coverage of employers.

Corruption in the media can also be influenced by the lack of awareness of integrity and ethical standards. For instance, a survey conducted in 2011 by the Centre for International Media Ethics' (CIME) Media Ethics Survey shows that in Latin America countries, the most important problem that journalist seem to face is the fear of being fired for keeping to ethical standards and pressures from editors and superior for bias reporting in favor of an individual or political interest.

In countries of Africa, amongst the major reasons for the low professional standard is the lack of awareness about media ethics. In Asian countries, the problem seems to be that journalists do not think that ethics is very important. Low salary, the fear of job loss, and general lack of awareness all create enough grounds for corruption to grow in the media.

Chapter Ten

Forms of Corruption in the Media

Corruption in the media comes in different forms from cash bribes in exchange for news coverage, fake news, nepotism and coverage in favor of political or private interests. It can also extend to the abuse of confidence or position in the hiring or disengagement of staff or when making a decision on the publishing news item or story, which can, in the end, affect the information that citizens consume.

1. Bribery

It is not unusual to hear stories of editors and journalist receiving bribes in exchange for twisted facts, publishing fake or staged stories, or not publishing ones that could damage a powerful entity.

According to the International Public Relations Association (IPRA), this is a widespread practice in Eastern Europe and Latin America. In a survey carried out by the organization, it was revealed that 60% of those who responded believed that paid articles are featured in editorials and not under advertisement.

Also, the story published by a media house might be influenced by the offer of a bribe to get more facts for the story or publish misleading and false information or changing the media coverage of an event to favor a party or put another at a disadvantage. Practices like these reduce the integrity of the media and results in the widespread circulation of "fake" or biased news

Cash for news coverage occurs at different levels all around the world:

• Interpersonal level: Cash is given to the journalist directly by the person who wants to be favored by the story

• Intra-organizational level: The higher-ups (editor) instructs the journalist on what to and what not to write. This could be as a result of management pressure to increase advertising

• Inter-organizational level: Here, there is a kind of arrangement in which an organization pays a news agency to publish some articles about it on an agreed schedule. In some countries such as Ukraine, China, or Russia, this arrangement can often be a bit of formal and might even have a legal contract as backing.

2. Gifts

The giving of gifts and advert placements are also ways by which the media can be compromised or influenced to cover stories that favor private or political interests. In developing countries where the salaries are low, journalists tend to give in more to this temptation than their counterparts in developed nations. This kind of corruption occurs a lot when PR agencies, ad agencies, and media houses collude. Sometimes, corruption in the media manifests itself in the form of advertisements which are not openly declared as such and are intentionally done that way to skew readers' perception and give favorable coverage to interest. For example, a news agency may report that a company is growing more robust and capturing more and more of the market while making the story appears independent and objective when in fact it is not.

Quite similar to this is the practice of passing paid advertisement as editorial comment or opinion. In Ukraine, for instance, this practice is known as "jeansa" and can even go on to include TV packages of news and whole program, articles, and even covers.

Concealed advertisement can also happen for political reasons in the case whereby a political party or candidate succeeds in influencing a media organization. For instance, in the parliamentary elections of Armenia in 2007, there were widespread cases of media bias and hidden advertising.

According to a report released by Yerevan Press Club which made public the bias in the coverage of the activities of some of the candidates. *"In some materials on the campaign events of opposition parties there were elements of irony, which were not reflected in the quantitative indicators of monitoring, but they impacted on the perception of the information by the audience."* Despite this claim, the same pattern was still observed in the 2008 presidential election campaign of the country.

3. Nepotism

The hiring or firing of staff for the publication of a feature is another way the media shows its corruption and consequently causes a distortion in the news that people consumed.

In countries where the government has the power to appoint the key staff of media houses, there is always the tendency for such powers to be misused. Positions are often given to friends, allies, and even family members, further ensuring that such administrations get a favorable report in the media.

4. Media Capture

Because mass media are very important source of information dissemination to citizens, they are often an outstanding asset in the manipulation of public opinion to favor personal or political interests. In many countries, where media capture is not present, it is latent. Media capture can involve cash for coverage as seen in Peru during the reign of Alberto Fujimori. It can also be seen in another level when the owner of a media house can use subtle and indirect influence to favor administrative or legislative actions concerning the media in his/her favor.

In the case of developing countries where the patronage system is deeply entrenched, the media may not be able to easily break free when it is tied down by clientele's patterns.

Fighting Corruption

The fight against corruption in the media can involve the use of different strategies from increasing the awareness of ethical standards in the industry to offering the press more freedom by setting up policies that support this. Hence, making the media more accountable for increased oversight and controls while giving support to investigative journalism by providing technical training.

1. Good legal framework:

For the fight against corruption in the media to yield substantial fruit, the adequate legal framework must be put in place. These frameworks should also be implemented in such a way that they guarantee the right to information and media freedom according to article 19 of the UN Covenant on Civil and Political Rights. Reviews of the rules and regulation that stifle the extent to which the right to information can be exercised should also be conducted. Such things as restrictive libel laws, tiresome and complicated registration and licensing should be reviewed so that journalists are protected from physical harm, inappropriate legal punishment, and political arbitrariness.

This is even more important for societies that are transiting to democracy since press freedom is a vital part of this system of government. Press freedom can be promoted by:

• Removing censorship and protecting freedom of expression

• Providing free access to government information

• Allowing journalist to protect their sources and whistleblowers

• Allowing transparency in the administration of media houses and agencies especially in the areas of ownership, registration, and taxation.

2.   Transparent Ownership:

Media pluralism should be encouraged by allowing the growth of competitive media companies. Any country that wants to fight corruption in the media must understand that there is a need to pull from state-controlled media as that makes it easy for the government to spread propaganda and distort public opinion.

Reports have shown that countries that have significantly cut down the size of state-controlled media have enjoyed a tremendous improvement in the size and quality of news coverage.

An example could be found in the case of Mexico where the news coverage of corrupt government officials increased following the government's privatization of the media in 1989. Irrespective of ownership, whether public or private, media owners must understand that their duty is to the people and journalists too must push for this in their duties. They must ensure that the principles of editorial independence adhere too.

Legislation that addresses conflict of interest must also be enacted to ensure that media ownership does not get in the way of freedom of information.

The International Federation of Journalist notes that new funding models that uphold the kind of journalism that has the public interest at the core should be explored. For these values to be supported and promoted so that the quality of journalistic reporting can be held high, proper attention should be paid to raising good professional and ethical standards. These measures should also include transparency in the ownership and political affiliations of media houses.

3. High Professional Standards

The bar needs to be raised when it comes to the level of journalism in developing countries. This can be achieved through proper technical and ethical training. Counterparts from the more developed region should also synergize in ensuring that issues of corruption are brought to light and addressed. In all of this, the civil societies also play a role in speaking out in defense of journalists who are assailed for exposing corrupt acts and practices. Training in investigative techniques should also be carried out. It is well-known the kind of physical risks and obstacles that journalists face when they go after top government officials or influential organizations. Therefore, it makes sense then that investigative journalism training should address risks and security issues.

Besides all of these, it's the duty of a journalist to be properly aware of the laws of the country in which they are reporting, particularly those that relate to media policies. When journalists are better trained, they will be better able to exercise their rights and know their limits. In Brazil, there is a group, Abraji which teaches journalist how they can exercise their rights when reporting.

There is also the issue of proper and adequate salary packages which ensures that journalists can work independently without compromising ethics for cash bribes or gifts.

Other Recommendations

International media communities and bodies should also work on:

• Raising awareness on the issue of corruption in the media through the regular holding of summit while inviting stakeholders in the PR industry and anti-corruption experts

• Acknowledging that corruption poses a problem, by publishing reports that documents or research on corruption in the media.

• Revealing to the public the pay level of journalists around the world.

Media development organizations should:

• Work on promoting ethics as an integral part of professional journalism with particular focus and training on cash for news coverage.

• Set up structure that makes the media accountable through transparency of operations

Owners of media agencies and editors should:

• Implement, follow, and promote a no-tolerance policy for any form of cash for coverage which could be a "harmless" encouragement payment to a journalist or paid advertisement clouded as an editorial viewpoint. This could mean that a structure or policy can be put in place to purge the system of whatever incentive will make a journalist engage in this practice.

• Accept that there is a relationship between salary and ethical standard

• Create a system that ensures transparency in operations and reporting to audiences.

PR professionals and their organizations should:

• Admonish members to adhere to zero tolerance for corruption and decline the offer of cash for coverage.

Chapter Eleven

Corruption and the Entertainment Industry

Corruption is not only in the domain of politicians and public officials, but it also extends into entertainment. The music business, for instance, is one that is mainly known for corrupt dealings and unspoken scandals. There are allegations of bribery, exploitation, scams, fraud, and shortcuts in print media and particularly on social media. The entertainment industry just like any industry that is motivated by profit also falls short when it comes to ethical standards.

1. Payola

In the music industry, for instance, the most common form of corruption is payola. Payola can be said to be *"the unreported payment to, or acceptance by, employees of broadcast stations, program producers, or program suppliers of any money, service, or valuable consideration to achieve airplay."* Payola has been happening in the music business for a long time and was legally criminalized in 1960.

In the '70s, the music industry of United States witnessed one of the biggest scandals in history. At the center of the storm was the president of CBS Records, Clive Davis. The scandal involved a lot of embellishment, payola, fraud, and even connections to crime syndicates. In Los Angeles, Davis had hired a man by the name of David Wynshaw as a sales representative. David Wynshaw had ties with Patsy Falcone who is connected to the Genovese Family, a West Coast Crime syndicate. Falcone functioned as the manager for music artists such as O.C Smith, Ben Vereen, Lynn Anderson, and Tommy Cash.

Under the direction of Clive Davis, Wynshaw and Falcone created fake companies that received payment worth over $75,000. Both men would create false invoices so that CBS would pay for expensive parties, jewelry, apartments and so on.

After Falcone's eventual arrest on charges related to drug trafficking, some of his earnings were tracked and led to the eventual arrest of Wynshaw. The arrests of both men put Clive Davis in the spotlight, and he was eventually arrested when the fake invoices were found to the tune of $94,000. Clive Davis was finally fired from his position.

In the investigation, Wynshaw revealed to investigators that CBS records have a sum of $250,000 every year that the company has set aside for payola to radio stations. When IRS began to audit the books of a CBS affiliate known as Philadelphia International in 1973, it found that CBS has been involved in payola in the form of quarterly checks for promotion. The checks revealed the person to whom the money was paid, the amount paid, and the time the money was paid. The report showed that all these happened with Clive Davis' knowledge. It was also revealed that the executives of CBS received over $340,000 in bribes from some retailers who were selling below the standard listing price to stores. The money received from these retailers was then used to pay-off radio stations who were promoting CBS.

It is important to note at this point that payola is a misdemeanor offense and attracts a $10,000 fine, plus a year in jail in the US. But despite this, no one has hardly served jail time for the offense; an indication that the law is rarely enforced to its full extent. A reason could be that the law itself isn't that high. For instance, the 1979 statutes state that social exchanges occurring between friends are not payola. This makes it difficult to prosecute payola with many record companies devising new ways to evade the grappling of the law. For example, it is not unusual to see record companies firing some of their promotion department staff (who are responsible for the payola) to avoid being investigated or losing the broadcast license. As soon as this is done, the organization will then engage the service of a new independent promoter that is not under the "supervision or control" of the organization. Some of them also avoid being investigated by making artists sign a contract that makes them obligated to promote their records. This way the managers of these artists lose money.

Payola still has a dangerous presence in the music industry and occurs in the US and other countries in some forms. South Korea has been making efforts in tackling payola scams, bribing of newspaper editors for positive reviews, embezzlement, purchase of video clip packages, and the practice of offering stock option in exchange for artist play, fake music chart on record sales, and public votes and links to organized crime by record company owners and other key players in the music industry.

In Hong Kong, over 20 executives of Universal Music were arrested on allegations of bribes of advantages, including money paid to the biggest TV station so that Universal Music artists can receive awards at the station's award show.

2. Royalty fraud

There is also the allegation of musicians being defrauded by record companies either in album sales revenue or the contract of engagement signed by both parties. Sometimes, the terms of the contract are scandalous and fraudulent, with the record companies capitalizing on the naivety of the artist during contract signing.

Some common practices of record companies include making the artist obligated for the payment of some parts of the record deal or withholding some part of the artist's royalty fees.

For instance, there is a process laid down by distribution companies and record companies to enable artists to get their royalties for music sales in retail stores. What happens is that the distribution companies give the master recording of the music tracks to duplication businesses that then duplicate the track and send it to each record store at their request.

The idea is that these record stores can return their shipments of the recordings to get a refund from the distributor which in this case is the record label. Now the record label will not pay all the full amount of the artist's royalty till it gets the refund from the distribution company. What this means, therefore, is that the distribution company holds on to money before they send it to the record label and before it eventually gets to the artist.

In many unethical cases, the record label will not truthfully report the number of records returned or kept by the distribution company to continue holding on to more money.

3.   Clear and clean

Record companies also engage in corrupt practices by changing the real figures of the number of documents that they sold for an artist's work. In the industry, this is known as bright and clean.

A bright refers to a record that does not reflect in the books for the reason of bootleg international shipping. It is a common practice for record labels to record sales figures that are lesser in number to the actual amount sold. What the label does is bootleg the master copy of the work without the barcode and ship it off to countries where the barcode system isn't used to track sales. Of course, since there are no record sales tracking system in place, the money does not show up on the books when the time for an audit comes.

A clean happens when records excessively produced are returned in access to the record company for cash without any scrutiny. The dishonest way how that works: records are given to vendors who will deliberately not pass these records to the retail store but will return it to the record label for a refund. The process puts money in the pocket of whoever is in charge of these private vendors.

The schedule of royalty is another way by which record companies scam artists. Royalties are paid on pay period, and this depends on when the record company takes delivery of the albums.

It is not unusual for record companies to hold artist royalties for as high as four pay periods to make return and shipping deductions from the account of the artist. These deductions are about twenty to forty percent of gross sales on reserve clauses.

For instance, on a thirty percent reserve, the record company takes thirty percent of the royalties and puts them in a bank so that they get interested in it for two years of not paying the artist while the record company keeps making more and more money off the royalties.

4. Exploitation

Artistes themselves are also capable of committing acts of corruption too by exploiting producers. Before the master recording is ready to be duplicated, the producer must sign off together with the artist that they both agree that the song is reproduced and distributed. If the producer refuses to sign-off on this and the artist goes ahead to duplicate, he/she will be committing a fraud under the copyright protection law that governs the activities of record companies, artists, and producers. But artists can cheat producers by re-recording the master that they both worked on.

Through the process of re-recording, the artist can remove the producer's right to the record. Where in a standard contract, the producer is entitled to receipt of payment if his tapes are used in a recording. An artist can bypass all that just by re-recording the song with the exact arrangement since copyright protection does not extend to musical arrangements. The producer could do all they can to sue the artist, but it will be an expensive waste of time and money as it is quite hard to prove.

5. Government propaganda

Corruption in entertainment not only applies to the music industry, but also the movie industry. In April of

2015, WikiLeaks, the online whistleblower organization led by Julian Assange released over 30,000 documents and 173,000 emails involving industry giant, Sony. The hack contains over 200,000 files from Sony Pictures Entertainment.

At the time of the release of the document, many wondered what made WikiLeaks (which usually exposes government corruption) go after Sony Pictures, an entertainment company. WikiLeaks published a statement on that saying, *"The Sony Archives show that behind the scenes, this is an influential corporation, with ties to the White House (there are almost 100 US government email addresses in the archive), with an ability to impact laws and policies, and with connections to the US military-industrial complex."*

Even though Sony fired back with a press release that seriously disagrees with WikiLeaks that the material is published publicly, it didn't deny that the company works directly with the US government.

Julian Assange had written that *"This archive shows the inner workings of an influential, multinational corporation. It is newsworthy and at the center of a geopolitical conflict. It belongs in the public domain. WikiLeaks will ensure it stays there."*

One of the most famous documents in the leak is one between Sony and the Democratic Party. In the email thread, the Democratic Party planned to create collections within the company so that the $5,000 ceiling on corporate campaign donations could be bypassed and donations could get to $50,000 to elect the New York Governor Andrew Cuomo.

A part of the email reads that, *"$50k is a heavy lift since most of it needs to come from individual contributions (only $5k can come from corp.), but I recommend we do it. . . I think we can get to the 50k commitment by making this a focus of our individual giving from execs this year."*

Another email released relates to the popular movie, *The Interview*. The email shows that a relationship exists between RAND, a part of the US-military-industrial complex and Sony pictures. The email explained that Sony tried to get advice from RAND on the movie and RAND linked up Sony with their analyst in the reclusive country, North Korea. The analyst then advised that Sony communicates with the US State Department and the NSA regarding what North Korea thinks.

To many people, the government through the CIA's Entertainment Industry Liaison Office uses Hollywood to advance its views and actions and make them more popular. For example, many believe that *The Interview* is propaganda of the US government under the cloak of political satire. The movie starred James Franco and Seth Rogen who are hired by the CIA to kill the North Korean president, Kim Jong-un. Many believe that the plan is to use humor to make viewers unsuspecting of violence while happy that an assassination has taken place. Little wonder why the North Koreans were not happy about the movie.

Tom Hayden explains in the LA Review of *Books* that the CIA promotes propaganda movies such as blockbusters like *Argo* and *Zero Dark Thirty* to create a good impression of itself through modern forms of entertainment.

Tony further explains that *"So true has the CIA–entertainment connection become, that few question its legal or moral ramifications. This is a government agency like no other; the truth of its operations is not subject to public examination. When the CIA's hidden persuaders influence a Hollywood movie, it is using a favorite medium to spin as favorable an image of itself as possible, or at least, prevent an unfavorable one from taking hold."*

Chapter Twelve

Corruption and Religion
Call for religion as a panacea

David Nussbaum, chief executive of Transparency International, in a 2006 speech at the London School of Economics, advocated for an approach to fighting corruption that takes into account the role played by personal values in making moral decisions as regards to corrupt practice. Nussbaum pressed further:

"In the case of value-based decisions like whether or not to bribe or accept a bribe, values and ethics can form a sort of threshold, establish under what emotional and external circumstances – if any – you may say yes. Your social environment, the level of trust you have in those around you, how you see this affecting the people you care about, will also come into play; but your values will be a fundamental guide in making these decisions"

Nussbaum advocated for religion as a tool against corruption because he thinks that there is a connection between personal values, religion, and corruption. It is a basic view of many people all around the world.

Because religion provides a sort of ethical standards to live by and rules that ensure that followers live a life of good morals, it has often been argued that religion can be a panacea for corruption. It is believed that in countries where religion is dominant and takes a firm hold, many citizens including public servants will for fear of going against the tenets of their religions keep to ethical practices and shun acts of corruption.

Calls for the use of religion and the *"fear of God"* in fighting against corrupt practices are becoming louder. For example, in Nigeria, public prayers are constantly being held by clerics and followers that "God puts his fear" in the leaders so that they can shun acts of corruption. They believe that the fear of God will make public servants deviate from their corrupt ways since they would not want to do what is in contrary to God's will. In Zamfara state, attempts have been made in the past to integrate local Islamic clerics into the civil service with the overall aim of reducing corruption and improving ethical standards. At the presidential level, the country has also seen pastors of big churches contesting for the top positions at Abuja, the seat of the Nigerian government. The influence can be felt in Pakistan, India, and Middle East.

Similarly, in Zambia, the Vice-President of the country from 2003- 2004, Nevers Mumba who is also a pastor and televangelist also challenged the church to help the government in its fight against corruption. He was reported to have said that the church is obligated mandatorily to help the government in its anti-corruption crusade.

In Uganda, the government also sought the help of the church in fighting acts of corruption. In 2006, a message delivered on behalf of President Museveni by the Minister for Public Service called on the church to help fight against corruption. The Minister stated that the government cannot fight corruption alone and thus needs the help of the church which is a better platform to do that.

The increasing call for religion as a tool in fighting corruption arises from the belief that honesty and fairness are the fundamentals of many religions around the world. Therefore, it only makes sense logically to use religious leaders as foot soldiers in the crusade against corruption. According to Beets, two distinct assumptions are responsible for why religious leaders are being called upon to mobilize followers in the fight against corrupt practices.

The first of this hypothesis is that those who are devoted to the tenets of these religions will shun corrupt practices since it involves theft, disobedience to the law, selfishness, etc. which are all against the fundamentals of these religions.

The second assumption is that those who are not followers or adherent of any religion are more likely to get involved in corrupt practices since they do not have any religion to guide them.

What research has shown?

Despite all of these assumptions and beliefs, many of the world's most corrupt countries according to rankings by Transparency International are ironically the most religious ones. (According to indicators by the Pew Global Attitudes Project).

There are academic and experiential evidence (by citizens living in these countries) that support the fact that religion doesn't necessarily provide a solution to corruption.

In Latin America for example, Arruda notes that despite the fact that people are becoming more devoted to the Roman Catholicism, corruption continues to grow and remains unchallenged by religion. The author includes a saying in Latin America: *"el que no tranza no Avanza"* (One that does not act unethically does not succeed), to illuminate the perversion of corrupt practices in the region.

What this means is that anyone that plans to succeed in business must be ready to get their hands dirty irrespective of their religious beliefs.

Mitchell supports an argument similar to that, considering the Philippines, where in a highly-religious country, corruption is exceedingly high. The author writes, *"From Presidents to prostitutes, religion flows like a river through Philippine lives, offering a bizarre mix of old style faith and sometimes bloody violence… In the Philippines, it seems, religion is never far away. At Easter, it bludgeons the imagination. Catholic worshippers in several towns re-enact the death of Christ by allowing themselves to be nailed to wooden crosses with stainless steel spikes. Other Filipinos descend in their millions on the nation's cathedrals and city squares to partake in a great upheaval of holy activity- preaching, praying, singing, dancing, kneeling and bowing.*

Even with all the public display of religiosity, corruption is still a grave issue. In the same vein, Beets notes that even though Scandinavian countries are secular with many of them experiencing declining religious influence, the effects of corruption are still very minimal especially when compared to those that are highly religious. It is also worthy to note that according to the Transparency

International Corruption Perception Index, Scandinavian countries are amongst the least corrupt.

Beets then attempts to explain this observation: in developing countries, the majority are the victims of corruption while the minority are the perpetrators. The majority then turns to religion to find solace.

Other explanations for this observation include the result of some research which shows that the tenets of the religions in some of these countries with high corruption rates may encourage followers to accept authority; a thing that might hinder attempts to prosecute corrupt public officials.

Now this kind of submission reflects in the cultural norm of hierarchy and structure in the family, school, and workplace, showed that blind loyalty is a common trait of religions with hierarchical structures such as Catholic, Eastern Orthodox, Hinduism, Sikhism, and Muslim. The work also shows that there is a correlation between this loyalty, greater corruption and tax evasion, reduced participation in civic activities and professional associations, higher inflation, and less efficient judiciaries.

Although there is no causal relationship between religion and corruption, there is, however, evidence that shows that a discursive relationship exists between all these three. This is very important because it can convince people to act in a certain way or avoid some certain behaviors.

If the followers of a religion and their adherents believe that they are religious, stand on a higher moral ground, and therefore less corrupt, than those who are irreligious, then this could affect the way they behave.

It is a common practice for religious leaders to urge their followers to shun corrupt practices. For instance, at the World Assembly of the World Council of Churches which was held in 1998, the organization urged its member churches to pressure a government to take legislative action against the different forms of corruption. Besides, in many countries, religious and faith-based organizations have been doing a very active job of being vocal about corruption.

Because they appear to be custodians of integrity and because of their extensive presence and reach, religious organizations, religious leaders, and networks together offer a powerful force in improving the standard of governance as it relates to development.

Even though there have been many hardworking and courageous religious leaders around the world who have all in one way or the other spoken out against corruption, there are still many religious organizations out there who have fallen to the trappings of corruption. For instance, in 2009, a priest was arrested for selling temple jewel at the world's largest Hindu temple at Tirupati. Also in the same year, some religious leaders were vocal against corruption in Ghanaian churches. In Nigeria, various allegations of misappropriation are leveled against pastors, for flamboyant lifestyles achieved by the diversion of church offerings into the private pockets.

There are numerous examples from around the world where the faith has been soiled and has been found wanting. The arrests of Ram Rahim, Rampal, and Assa Ram, the top three religious gurus in recent years explain the connection between religion and corruption. They played a card of faith to fulfill their inner desire for money, sex, and power. Therefore, it is understandable when the call for religious leaders to increase the fight for corruption is severely weakened by the corruption happening in religious institutions.

There hasn't been any proof that religion brings about corruption or the lack of it and certainly not with all the current methodologies that have been used so far on the subject.

What seems to be the case is that there is the possibility

that religion can be used to change the discourse around corruption. In many countries of the world, religion is an important part of the people's behavior, attitude, and values, which therefore makes it an important source of power and a veritable instrument of influence.

The way forward would be for religious leaders and faith-based organizations to ensure that they carry their adherents and followers along in the fight against corruption.

In addition to this, what is considered as corruption in many countries needs to be spelled out. As Gupta notes that *"the discourse of corruption varies a great deal from one country to another, dependent as it is on particular historical trajectories and the specific grammars of public culture."* In Nigeria, as Smith noted, *"When Nigerians talk about corruption, they refer not only to the abuse of state offices for some private gain but also to a whole range of social behavior in which various forms of morally questionable deception enable the achievement of wealth, power, or prestige as well as more mundane ambitions. Nigerian notions of corruption encompass everything from government bribery and graft, rigged elections, and fraudulent business deals, to the diabolical abuse of occult powers, medical quackery, cheating in school, and even deceiving a lover.*" In Northern Nigeria, adultery, and prostitution are also seen as acts of corruption which is why Sharia law is implemented in a state like Zamfara as a response to curb these kinds of corrupt practices that the standard Nigerian law does not recognize.

Even in Zambia, a favorite newspaper, the Times of Zambia reported that the Vice-President, Mumba, encouraged the church to take a stand against practices which are unethical. The headline of that newspaper report was: *"Zambia gets 'tough on corruption."*

Therefore, the definition of what constitutes corruption amongst other things is fundamental if religion is going to be used to change the discourse around corruption.

Chapter Thirteen

Corruption and Research

The case of research fraud involving Japanese scientist, Dr. Haruko Obokata in 2014 is a prime example of corruption in scientific research. Before the controversy, Obokata worked as a researcher at the Riken Center for Development Biology in Japan. Riken is among the list of the top prestigious institutes of research in Japan. At Riken, Obokata researched on stem cells.

In the medical science community, research into stem cells gets a lot of attention because of its possibility of use in the repair and replacement of damaged body organs. Obokata went on to publish her findings in the reputable and well-respected science journal, Nature. She published two papers including effortless and easy-to-follow new way of producing a large number of stem cells. The publication got massive attention as expected. In fact, many in the medical community called it revolutionary. She became very famous as a result of the research and even granted TV interviews.

Of course, since stem cell research gets a lot of attention as mentioned earlier, it is only normal for other scientists to replicate her methods to see if they will get the same results and arrive at the same conclusion. But this was not so, as they all were not successful. This cast doubts on the authenticity of her research and the truthfulness of her findings. In science, the inability to reproduce an experiment and get the same result each time means the analysis is invalid!

Because doubts about the authenticity of her claims started to grow, local investigations were conducted, and the results only made the situation darker for Dr. Obokata.

After local studies had proved her wrong, extensive investigations followed, with none favoring her position on the new method of stem cell production that she has worked on. Through it all, the scientist maintained her position that her research was genuine but she was unable to explain to her peers why her work has not been successfully duplicated.

In the middle of the storm, coworkers at Riken, supervisors and even other researchers were questioned, to ascertain the truth of the entire situation. In the end, Obokata was given the opportunity to duplicate her published lab results under the strict supervision of scientists. She did this for eight long months at the end of which all the results she achieved were negative. As a result of this, after about two years of being investigated by institutions and government agencies, she was found guilty of misconduct in research.

As a punishment, her published papers in the top journal, Nature, was retracted. She resigned from her job and was fined. Her supervisor and higher-ups were seriously reprimanded even though they were not directly found guilty of misconduct. Her direct supervisor, who couldn't bear the shame, sank into depression and eventually committed suicide at the age of 52. Riken underwent a major restructuring as staff was fired and new management was constituted to direct the affairs of the institute. The government also issued a revised standard for the conduct and misconduct of research in the country.

Causes of corruption in research

For many people, the case of Dr. Obokata's (she eventually had her Ph.D. withdrawn over plagiarism) disregard for ethics and involvement in data manipulation and fabrication. All happens due to the overbearing pressure on scientists and researchers to come up with something new, publish something innovative and exciting in reputable journals—all in a bid to get more research funding or boost career prospects.

Now, this pressure is not cultural because it extends to many academic institutions whether in the United States, Japan, China, or Russia. There are many examples of plagiarism, data manipulation, failure to include co-authors, and failure to properly reference used works in many institutions of the world. The only difference is that there are more cases of these academic frauds in some countries than others.

In 2010, Nature, for instance, noted that fraud in Chinese research is on the increase. Reported in a survey by the Chinese government, about a third of over 6000 researchers at top six institutions in the country, admitted to plagiarism, falsification, or fabrication. Two years later, a top American journal, Proceedings of the National Academy of Sciences, released a study of retractions based on the country from which they originated. The authors wrote that for articles on PubMed, a first medical repository in the US, there were more retractions from China and India than from the US. The study also found that by retractions due to duplication (duplication here refers to the same research paper published in many journals), China was the number one in the world. By retraction due to fraud, Japan was number one, followed by Germany, US, and China.

To some people, the people who are to blame for research fraud are not the scientists, rather the administrators who have imposed a culture of "publish or leave" in research institutions. These officials include senior people in the universities and research funders. The way universities PR also exaggerate claims also puts scientist under undue pressure to give the hungry media something new to feast on. In an internet article by Guardian, it was reported that the medical department of Imperial College was given a "productivity target" which is to publish at least three research papers every year with one in a prestigious journal and an impact factor of at least five. The effect of this kind of pressure is all too glaring as it forces the scientist to be under unnecessary pressure and temptation to meddle in unethical practice to meet the set target number of research papers.

The only field where everyone knows that the pressure to publish something can be beneficial is the publishing industry. Pressure to publish in science only leads to sloppy work and unethical practice.

When it is not compelled to release, it is the pressure to manipulate data to publish some specific studies with some specific outcomes based on the dictates of the people funding the studies. What this means is that if a company wants to publish a particular result, all they need to do is, pay a scientist to look at that result by whatever means, even if it comes at the expense of the integrity of such a study.

Now conducting a study where the outcome is already predetermined is known as P-Hacking. And this involves the collection of a vast number of variable and then manipulating the data until a result that is relatively close to the desired outcome is achieved. Even though statistically-speaking, the result could make sense, but in practicality, it will be utterly meaningless. Now making this predetermined conclusion appear like it is made from a real scientific method of evaluation, can be achieved through different means such as, the use of small sample sizes, the overreliance on as a test subject such as mice and concluding that it holds true for humans too, data manipulation such as inclusion and exclusion or rearrangement to support the presupposition of the researcher.

Another reason why some scholars engage in fraud is money. Although money received, in this case, is not like politicians where money is spent on luxury lifestyles and stashed, but it is still an act of corruption. In most cases, money received goes into their professional coffers for the purchase of research equipment not covered by their grants, salaries of research assistants and coworkers, business traveling expenses, expensive software for research, etc.

For a researcher to do quality research, some of this equipment and tools are necessities and not luxuries. Therefore, it is understandable why some fall for this temptation.

But the consequences of dishonesty in research are far-reaching even to the point that it betrays the trust of the public on an entire body of knowledge. As seen in the case of Obokata:

- There is a significant cost in time and effort to prove the truth and reach a verdict especially when the researcher at the center of the storm maintains consistently that experimental results are real and valid. However, it means that time and resources have to be allocated to prove the alleged perpetrator wrong.

- Investigations into cases of research fraud always expand to include collaborators, supervisors, reviewers, coworkers, editors, and the institution where research was conducted

• After a verdict has been reached and it is one that pronounces the researcher guilty, everyone involved gets soiled. Supervisors, institutions, and the entire body of knowledge.

• Even though reforms in the ethical standard are usually recommended and in many cases put in place, they don't usually get as much coverage as the scandal, and in many cases, even the underlying cause of the scandal is not addressed.

Acts of dishonesty destroy the integrity of a field and the practical ability of other researchers to go ahead and continue from there. They believe a truthful research has ended when designing their new research experiments.

When a researcher through dishonesty acquires a research grant, they are hindering directly the chance of another honest researcher in getting funding for a good and worthy project. This is a very important scenario in the discussion of corruption in research.

Solution

The way forward in reducing corruption as it pertains to research is to focus attention and reforms on the severe pressure faced by scientists researching modern universities. Pressures such as getting more research grant money, research publications, experimental results, breakthroughs, etc.

Even though many may argue that they are KPIs (Key Performance Indicators) and are needed to track the progress and productivity of academics as employees of institutions, they are a constant source of concern. The inability to scale through these hurdles will mean negative consequences for the career of any scientist. If the actual cause of corruption is not addressed, the problem will only persist and even increase. Obokata was just unlucky, and many other cheaters are never caught as the pressure to be dishonest remains there throughout their entire career.

Chapter Fourteen

Corruption and Immigration

Corruption and migration are similar on several fronts. First of all, they play important roles in the process of development of any country. Secondly, they are always on the policy agendas of countries. Lastly, global discussion on both has reached epic proportion in the last decades.

Nonetheless, the relationship between both, whether in the country of origin or around migration territories is one that hasn't been seriously explored. The relationship between both has grave implications for all the players involved: migrants, communities in which immigration or emigration is taking place, policymakers, as well as practitioners. Even though in the discussion of migration, it rarely pops up, corruption is still an issue that still today affects people's life and plays a role in why they migrate.

The relationship between corruption and migration is one that goes both ways. Movement can play a part in the perception and actual practice of corruption. In the same way, corruption can inspire, enable, or inhibit migration. Corruption can also shape the effects of migration on a country. When people migrate, there is a mix of ideas about what constitutes corruption and what does not. Immigration is not only for destination countries but also the case in communities where people migrate from. This is because those who have migrated, acquired different perspectives, and still retaining their transnational ties, they tend to transfer these aspects to their originating community.

Countries, where corruption is believed and perceived to be rampant, are usually those of immigration.

The causes and effect of migration-corruption relationship are crisscrossed in the pattern.

Here are a few:

1. Corruption causes illegal immigration:

Disregard for the law, regulations, and ethics induces bribery. And as far as bribery is concerned, migration is not immune. It is not unheard of for corrupt officials to generate fake travel documents, care little for human trafficking, and even offer protection to chief perpetrators of human trafficking. When all of these happen, corruption stands as a blockade against the due process of migration management. This is one of the most glaring instances of the effect of corruption in migration.

The converse of the point is that people who are afraid of being persecuted in their country often rely on corruption to get protection from another country.

Many countries in Europe, for example, seriously enforce policies that reduce the number of people seeking asylum in their countries. One of such measures is that they make it very difficult to even get to their borders in the first place. But what is interesting is the fact that highly-organized human-trafficking rings which depend on corrupt immigration officials usually offer the safest ways to travel. This is because they can use bribes to get very well-forged travel documents that can guarantee travel through the normal means.

2.   Corruption creates a blockade for the inherent benefits of migration:

Migration has its natural benefits such as the alleviation of poverty, promotion of national development for instance through the transfer of economic ideas & development initiatives by citizens in a diaspora, and investment by migrants.

Corruption prevents the utilization of these potential benefits as seen when people in trusted positions in the country of origin mismanage and siphon remittances by these migrants.

If bribery takes place during the acquisition of a license to operate a building, multiple taxations in running a business to mention a few, migration-driven investment will be significantly reduced.

Also, if the people receiving the remittance are targeted for extortion, the migrants will refuse to send money home, and investment will reduce significantly.

Corruption can also inhibit the return of highly-skilled migrants back to their country of origin as seen in the case of developing countries where there are no structures to absorb these skilled people. This can happen in a system that is rigged with nepotism. If for instance, people at the helms of affairs, back home decide to choose relatives and friends over merit in job interviews or contract bidding process, migrants will not leave a merit-based system for this.

It is common for many highly skilled migrants to want to go back home to develop their own countries, but if the system creates a blockade for this to happen, they will be frustrated, demoralized, and unwilling to return—a recipe for underdevelopment in the origin country.

3.   Corruption induces the desire to migrate:

When citizens start losing faith in the system, they will often look to other countries for opportunities. When corruption and nepotism hold meritocracy to ransom, residents will be forced to react by moving elsewhere, especially those who are highly skilled. A situation is known as brain drain. Widespread corruption hinders economic development and dispensation of justice. The resulting poverty and insecurity can inspire the wish to migrate.

4.   Corruption increases the demand for transnational ties amongst the wealthy:

In countries where corruption perception is high, the wealthy minority are the ones who usually benefit from cross-border ties. Money from corrupt dealings ensures that international migration happens even when it is to countries with no apparent benefit to them or the country of origin. The corrupt rich often see international travel as an opportunity to launder money or keep their possessions out of the reach of other citizens who might demand accountability. Many also do this as a sort of backup plan against prosecution. In China, for instance, it is common for corrupt and powerful officials to send their children abroad along with money as an insurance against a change in fortune.

5.   Corruption does not encourage return:

Many migrants upon arrival experience culture shock and most of the time prefer entrepreneurship over paid employment. There is also the challenge of re-establishing a livelihood all over again. If migrants have adapted and learned to live in a society of less corruption in their destination country, they may want to distant themselves from the country of origin if corruption is pervasive. Bribe requests by immigration personnel at the border have been found to frustrate short visits home and hence makes the thought of settling down demotivating.

For long-term resettlement, corruption can seriously hamper the process of floating a business, therefore, make economic integration very difficult for returnees.

6.   Social remittances bring corruption down:

Social remittances are the norms and values that

migrants who maintain close ties to home transfer to the people close to them in their country of origin. Since people typically move from highly corrupt countries to those with lower corruption rate, over time, they tend to become critical of corrupt practices in their home country and therefore attempt to spread the anti-corruption message in their country of origin.

Nonetheless, this is a two-way thing as citizens of highly corrupt nations can bring with them corrupt practices when they enter destination countries. If this happens on a big scale, then it might upset the social model in the destination country.

7.   Migration upset social structures:

Migration changes the country of origin socially. Where in the past landowners and corrupt elite including public official hold power in the country of origin, migrants through their transnational tie can shoot their own families and other individuals in the major positions. Such changes might upset the structure of nepotism in the system and create a positive effect.

Migration produces social changes that may eradicate corruption. In the reverse scenario, cash remittance by diaspora citizens can give rise to new forms of corruption.

8.   Migration can improve corruption:

This can happen in the destination country. If the people who migrate from highly corrupt countries begin to display acts of corruption or start to protest against what they think it is unacceptable, it can deprive the destination country the opportunity of having voices that will protest against corruption.

9.   Corruption makes it difficult for migrants to receive assistance:

In settings where corruption is high, aid to migrants may be faced with obstacles in several ways. The most obvious way is the diversion, and embezzlement of funds which tend to reduce the effectiveness of such aid programs.

Cases in point:

• Nigeria: Human Trafficking and corruption

In Nigeria, there is a well-established human trafficking ring which targets Europe for the perpetuation of corruption. This ring has a large base in Edo state, in the Niger Delta region of Nigeria.

In the Nigerian case, corruption manifests itself in every stage of human trafficking from recruitment in Nigeria, transportation through the border, and long-term exploitation at destination countries. These human traffickers depend a lot on the giving of bribes to public officials to turn a blind eye to their illegal activities. Bribes are also given in exchange for original passports obtained illegally for the victims so they could travel abroad.

Nigeria is consistently listed as one of the most corrupt countries in the world where poverty is high despite the country being one of the richest in Africa. This means that institutions set up to cater for and protect the citizens are weak and ineffective. Such illegal activity flourishes because the participants: the traffickers and public officials enjoy the financial advantages.

The entire system allows the corrupt practices to permeate through it and gives rise to problems such as human trafficking.

- Iraq: Assisted Return and Corruption

Norway created the IRRINI program in 2008 to encourage Iraqi nationals who are asylum seekers to return home. IRRINI is the acronym for Information, Return, and Reintegration of Iraqi Nationals to Iraq.

The program was to offer free airfare to Iraq as well as the cash grant upon arrival, and the opportunity of in-kind assistance such as in setting up of businesses. The International Organization for Migration (IOM) implemented the program with more than 2,300 Iraqis returning to Iraq through the program as at 2015.

On closer inspection of the program, one will see several challenges including the effect of corruption in Iraq on the effectiveness of the program.

First of all, the cash grant was set up in Norwegian kroner but was eventually disbursed in US dollars and therefore waivered in value due to currency fluctuations. In a country where corruption is endemic, Iraqi returnees who received less than their counterparts quickly attributed the reduction to corruption.

Secondly, as part of the requirement in helping the returnees settle and start a business, IOM requested that quote for the cost of materials from three suppliers be submitted before assistance can be granted. This quickly became a challenge for some because getting the quote is not a part of the Iraqi business culture. On closer observation, it was found that some of these returnees paid money to get fabricated quotes from both real & fictitious business to set up fraudulent businesses so that they can get the in-kind assistance which they can convert to cash.

Thirdly, those who were able to get the right papers had to wait for feedback of verification from IOM headquarters which is not in Iraq. Therefore, the standard anti-corruption procedure hindered the swift delivery of service and assistance.

- Latin America: Corruption & remittance

Many Latin Americans migrate in search of more favorable opportunities as they send home, money to family and friends. While these monies can significantly improve the living and social conditions of those who receive them, it might also make them targets of corruption. For instance, through data obtained from Americas Barometer, in 24 countries in Latin America, a study investigated the connection between corruption (especially that of extortion by law enforcement officers) and the intention to migrate. The result showed that citizens who are averse to corruption expressed interest in migration. This indicates that corruption leads to morality drain.

Another investigation found that those who receive

remittances are more likely to be the targets of extortion and other forms of corruption as they are perceived to be wealthier. In many of these countries too, men are much more likely to be extorted than women. Individuals who are highly educated are even more liable to be extracted. The studies show how the potential benefits from migration can be hindered by corruption in the country of origin.

What could be done?

Fighting corruption as it relates to migration is very critical especially in putting an end to the reasons why people are leaving their homes in droves. Countries that rank high on mass migration: Turkey, Mexico, Greece, Croatia, Italy, Morocco, etc. must put in place proper anti-corruption standards that are by best practices globally and are enforced by the police and border officials.

Because of the fact these countries are already facing economic crisis and uncertainty, the additional strain of the refugee issue and aid money also carries the potential risk of corruption. Therefore, whenever financial assistance is required, anti-corruption provisions must be put in place and adhered to, to ensure that money is not wasted.

The international community should look into the best ways in which the actions of corrupt and criminal smuggling group can be seriously limited. This will require information gathering and data sharing across borders.

Political instability and lack of good accountable governance are top causes of the reason people risk everything to travel to developed countries. Therefore, there is a need to put in place policies that address these issues in the long term.

The United States Immigration Policy Under Donald Trump:

Immigration has been the hallmark of President Donald Trump's presidential campaign. As at the time of writing, it is still generating a lot of discussions all around the world for obvious reasons.

During the campaign, one of his most famous promise to voters was to build a wall along the US-Mexico border. He has also expressed support for a pause on the issuance of green cards and H-1B visas given to highly skilled immigrants.

Trump in his announcement speech stated that "When Mexico sends its people, they're not sending their best. They're not sending you. They're sending people that have lots of problems, and they're bringing those problems…They're carrying drugs. They're bringing crime.

They're rapists. And some, I assume, are real people."

Barely four months before the election, Trump released a written statement to make his position clearer. Part of the declaration read that "The Mexican Government is forcing their most unwanted people into the United States. They are, in many cases, criminals, drug dealers, rapists, etc. This was evident just this week when, as an example, a young woman in San Francisco was viciously killed by a 5-time deported Mexican with a long criminal record, who was forced back into the United States because they didn't want him in Mexico. This is merely one of the thousands of similar incidents throughout the United States. In other words, the worst elements in Mexico are being pushed into the United States by the Mexican government.

The largest suppliers of heroin, cocaine and other illicit drugs are Mexican cartels that arrange to have Mexican immigrants trying to cross the borders and smuggle in the drugs. The Border Patrol knows this. Likewise, the tremendous infectious disease is pouring across the border.

The United States has become a dumping ground for Mexico and, in fact, for many other parts of the world. On the other hand, many fabulous people come in from

Mexico and our country is better for it. But these people are here legally and are severely hurt by those coming in illegally. I am proud to say that I know many hard working Mexicans—many of them are working for and with me ... and, just like our country, my organization is better for it."

On January 27, 2017, the month he took over the mantle of leadership from Barack Obama, he signed an executive order which effectively banned citizens of six countries: Iraq, Iran, Libya, Somalia, Sudan, Syria, and Yemen from coming to the US for 90 days. The order also extended to refugees of the civil war in Syria who were indefinitely banned while refugees from other countries were banned for 120 days. The law was titled, "Protecting the Nation from Terrorist Attacks by Foreign Nationals."

The order quickly drew a backlash from many US citizens and those of other countries. By the end of 48 hours, more than 40 cases have been filed in the federal courts. Many courts granted temporary restraining order (TRO) that prevents the enforcement of some parts of the order.

A few weeks after the 0rder was restrained by the courts, the president, and his team revised it and excluded Iraq, green card residents, and visa holders from the ban.

Even though the president had consistently blamed the country's neighbor and one of the biggest trading partners, Mexico, for its increasing corruption and job losses, a study published by Social Science Quarterly has found that no evidence exists that proves that Mexican or illegal immigrants contribute to acts of corruption in the country. However, it found that a relationship exists between illegal immigrants and crimes.

Back and Forth relationship:

It is evident from the preceding on migration and corruption that both play a role in the cause and effect of one another. The effect that corruption has on migration is sometimes unpredictable. In fact, they could be contradictory. Migration can bring about a reduction in corruption in some ways and even amplify it in another.

Corruption can inspire the desire to migrate whether directly or not. The motivation can be so much that the individual will do anything to migrate in the face of harsh restrictive policies.

Because the relationship is two-ways, this presents another dimension to the already complicated relationship between them.

The concerns of the people migrating, destination countries, and countries of origin all show that it is important to fight corruption

Chapter Fifteen

Corruption and Drug Trafficking

In the discussion of transnational organized crime, drug trafficking always features prominently. On close observation, the effect of corruption in drug trafficking becomes evident. In an analysis conducted by the United Nations Office on Drugs and Crime (UNODC) in 2011, it was revealed that illicit drugs were the largest income source for transnational crime and accounts for about half the proceed from transnational crime and a fifth of all proceeds from criminal activities. In 2003, the UNODC estimated that the global illicit drug trade to be about $322 billion—a figure higher than the Gross Domestic Product of over 80 countries.

The corrupting effect of the illicit drug trade is mostly felt in drug-cultivating countries such as Mexico, Columbia, Guinea-Bissau, and Afghanistan. It is also evident in drug-transit countries such as Ecuador and Venezuela where organized criminal groups obtain massive wealth from the different forms of the drug trafficking trade.

Many times, a part of the proceeds were used to secure protection or request that corrupt public officials and law enforcement turn a blind eye to their activities. Many of these organized criminal groups often use extreme violence in their operations.

Corruption when it comes to drug-related activities occurs in several forms and degree of severity. The chief participants are often law enforcement, military, state and federal government, and the judiciary. Drug-related corruption causes decay in public institutions. If corruption is found in a system, i.e., law enforcement, it is usually found throughout the strata of the organization. New members are indoctrinated and taught corrupt practices. Drug-related corruption takes many forms.

- Protection from the enforcement of the law:

Here, Drug Trafficking Organizations (DTOs) receive protection from the law enforcement agents that are supposed to be hunting them and bringing them to book. Drug traffickers pay for protection by offering bribes which may be one-time for the passage of drugs or by schedule; a system that DTOs prefer and operate on. Often, the bribe is paid to top officials in the police or the military who then guarantee safe passage.

- Exoneration of criminal charges:

Most times, drug traffickers are caught, but usually, these are the bottom feeders; the mules who serve as the conduit for the shipment of drugs to delivery locations. Because the kingpins of these DTOs are often influential, they easily bribe their way through the maze of law enforcement and judicial process. They can circumvent the justice delivery system by bribing judges.

Violence is a hallmark of most DTOs. They carry out physical abuse and violent executions to bring those who stand in their way into submission. Therefore, it is common to find drug criminals threaten or coerce incorruptible judges and law enforcement agents.

On occasions when this seems to be difficult, they use their contacts in the police to tamper with evidence so that such cases are eventually turned away.

- Extralegal violence:

It is a common practice for law enforcement in drug-producing countries to resort to extra-judicial killings when they cannot arrest or charge drug criminals to court. Sometimes, corrupt law enforcement officials sympathetic to a drug cartel often execute members of other drug cartels instead of arresting them.

- Taking over criminal activity:

This happens when a civil servant runs their drug trade and use their position and influence to get immunity from detention and prosecution.

All of these forms of drug-related corruption are manifestations of a corruption-entrenched government. If a government is unable to enforce the law throughout of all its territories, then drug growers, traffickers, and dealers will carry out operations as they wish. These individuals will bribe public officials since they have to go through them. Drug dealers spend a lot bribing civil servants year-in-year-out. In Mexico, only bribery costs can be as high a billion dollars every year.

Cases in point:

Drug-related corruption is always present in any country that drug traffickers operate in. In drug-producing countries, corruption is found from the head of government institutions to the lowest member of staff especially in the custom. It is present at all levels. For countries which perform the role of transit, corruption occurs at the top levels of government and in law enforcement agencies. For consumer countries, corruption is usually at the law enforcement level.

1. Drug-related corruption in Colombia

Colombia has consistently topped the list of drug-producing countries of which there are about 20 countries. Corruption in Colombia exists at all levels of government. Colombia is the hub of drug traffickers. A look into the drug trafficking landscape of Colombia reveals a history that is shocking as well as enlightening.

In the 1980s, Colombia was the base of what's probably the most deadly and notorious drug syndicate in the history of the world, the Medellin Cartel, with Pablo Escobar as its leader. Escobar along with his brothers made so much money from the drug trade that they were featured in Forbes Magazine in 1987 as some of the richest people in the world.

Throughout the period, the Medellin cartel carried out attacks on prominent political figures who wanted the Colombian government to extradite drug criminals to the US. The attacks included kidnappings, bombings, and assassinations. Escobar was notorious for offering public officials a choice of plata o plomo ("silver or lead" or a bribe or a bullet).

Through this, he was able to bribe or threaten a lot of law enforcement agents making it very hard for anyone to build a criminal case against him. Escobar eventually went on to the campaign and got elected to the Colombian Parliament. One of the most notable bribes Escobar offered was to pay off the foreign debts of the Colombian government in exchange for a pardon for drug trafficking charges.

The government turned down the bribe, and Escobar was sent to jail in a private prison that was designed and built by him and one that he was free to go and come from. Escobar escaped from the prison after he was informed that he would be moved to a real prison. Shortly after that, he was killed in 1993 by a special anti-drug unit that was trained by US forces.

With Escobar out of the picture, the Cali Cartel, a rival group took over the drug trafficking scene and paid millions of dollars in bribe to government officials. Other groups such as the Revolutionary Armed Forces of Colombia (FARC) and the paramilitary group, the United Self-Defense Forces of Colombia (AUC) grew stronger and became more involved in the drug trade.

Estimates put the percentage of elected congress who drum support for the AUC at 35%. In 2010, the 87 members of congress, 15 governors, and 35 mayors were investigated for their connection to the paramilitaries.

A particularly disturbing case of police corruption were the Trujillo massacres where within the three years, government forces and drug traffickers carried out 100 assassinations. A prime example of extrajudicial killings.

2.   Drug-related corruption in Mexico

The government of Mexico at all levels has had a long history of amorous relationship with drug traffickers. During the reign of the Institutional Revolutionary Party, the Mexican government and the police acted as mediators amongst rival drug cartels. Government officials separated the country into plazas or areas of control which were sold to each cartel.

Doing this had two implications. First of all, it ensures that violence between cartels reduce as each has their territory. Secondly, it provides that a cartel does not become too big as smaller cartels are usually not able to buy the plazas. When power changed hands in 2000 with the election of Felipe Fox, a member of the National Action Party (PAN), the system was disrupted. After this,

Felipe Calderon, also a party member with Fox, started the war on drugs in Mexico. President Calderon increased military spending and troops deployed to the hotspots controlled by drug cartels in the country. A move which has yielded positive results.

A solution to drug-related corruption:

A solution to drug-related corruption can be found in the method adopted by the New York Police Department of the United States. Police corruption in the US is very rare and is therefore why this model comes recommended.

In the 1970s, corruption in the NYPD seems to be institutionalized especially with the increasing global drug trade at the time. The police set up two commissions to investigate corruption within the department and to make changes in policy that will ensure that corruption becomes a forgotten issue in the office. The policy changes by the Knapp and Mollen Commission seem to work because after the policy took effect, reports of corruption reduced and today, there is almost no story of corruption against the department in any news outlet.

In the 70s, Detective Frank Serpico blew the whistle on corruption in the department after he was ignored by his superior to whom he had reported the issue. Before that time, no one had given attention to corruption in the department. The incident shows the effect of independent media in fighting corruption in the government and the society as a whole.

Another case that highlights the usefulness of the media as a tool to stopping corruption is what happened in the Bahamas in the 80's. The US government had received information that the Prime Minister, Lynden Pindling and some members of his cabinet were taking bribes from drug cartels. After diplomacy couldn't be used as a negotiation tool, the US government leaked the information to the media. An action that caused the public to pressure the Prime Minister into investigating the issue.

Another example is the case of the US government cables released by WikiLeaks in January 2011. The cables showed the corruption within the ruling family in Tunisia. As a result of this, the Tunisians revolted in an uprising that led to the removal of President Ben Ali.

When the Knapp Commission started work, its policy focused on four major changes in the NYPD.

• Firstly, the commission put in place an accountability system that ensured that superiors were responsible for the actions of subordinates.

- Secondly, special undercover units carried out tests of integrity. The units will tempt officers in the field to make them commit crimes or accept bribes. No one knew who was a part of the team and where and when the test would occur.

- Thirdly, the Internal Affairs division was revamped and became feared.

- Lastly, any citizen that offered bribed was picked up and charged.

These policies were very efficient and reduced corruption to the barest minimum. Since then the department has been almost free of corruption, except for a few cases. It is worthy of note that the NYPD is the largest police department in the US.

Chapter Sixteen

Conclusion

The major global issues are the products of corrupt minds. Fighting against corruption is not limited to stopping cash transactions, but also harnessing everything that cash can buy. Most criminal and unethical practices are based on cash. Drug dealing, underworld, mafia, terrorism, kidnapping, illegal immigration, human trafficking, and fake media run their wheels on rolls of money.

Much can be achieved without using rules, regulations, courts, and other government hassles if we stop using cash.

Microsoft, Facebook, Twitter, Amazon, Google, Apple, and eBay are the top performing companies in the world, and all of them were started from a tiny room, cabin, or a garage. They all have a few things common; they kept their core values high without exploring the immoral or unethical options. They kept their dealings and transaction transparent, honest, candid, and simple. Most of them probably never used cash to build multi-billion-dollar institutions. They don't bribe people to buy their product or sign a government contract to become successful, but they use talent, expertise, innovation, breakthrough, and vision.

Fighting and ridding our society of corruption requires a combination of approaches as one single method is never enough. Many of these approaches have been discussed as they apply to different areas of human endeavor where corruption has taken hold. However, when one takes a closer look at the various manifestations of corruption, patterns begin to emerge, and it becomes immediately apparent that a single solution can be effective in blocking off the different ways in which corruption manifests itself.

One of such solution is a Cashless Society.

The governments of India and Nigeria, two of the countries which rank high on the Corruption Perception Index have ramped up the war against corruption by enacting the cashless policy. In India, the Prime Minister, Narendra Modi has implemented a currency policy that reduced the number of high denominations currencies in the move to cut "black money." A cashless society is that where currency notes or cash are not used in monetary transactions. The benefits of a cashless economy are huge.

Since cash is the primary instrument for most corrupt practices, a truly cashless society will discourage citizens from money laundering, financial misappropriation, budget inflation, etc.

Toward the tail end of the Obama administration in 2016, the US government flew over 400 million dollars' worth of cash in foreign currency to Iran as settlement of a failed trade deal in 1979, around the time the Shah fell. This drew a lot of controversy for many reasons. First of all, why was so much cash involved? Iran has been labeled a terrorist nation and one of the most corrupt countries in the world. Therefore, Americans were skeptical about the cash falling into wrong hands. If the cash falls into the hands of corrupt politicians, they would be used to sponsor terrorism.

Cash transactions are difficult to trace and present a large risk to the safety of the American people. In fact, the cash transfer was made on the same day Iran released four American prisoners and formally implemented the nuclear deal. Many saw it as cash for hostage situation even though the administration claimed otherwise. A simple solution would have been for both countries to leverage on a cashless policy system where the money can be transferred electronically, and the trails can be available for everyone to see and monitor.

A cashless society also reduces tax evasion because the economy is based on financial institutions leveraging on digital platforms—a setup that ensures transaction trails are available for government institutions and law enforcement agents to follow. Because stolen money often goes into real estate as evident amongst Indian politicians and drug lords in Latin America, the price of real estate will be reduced since the costs can no longer be inflated by these corrupt persons. Welfare programs will also start to experience a great efficiency in operations particularly in the disbursement of funds. Since funds will be transferred electronically, transaction details will become more transparent as payments can be easily traced and received.

A transparent transaction will ensure that records will not be manipulated and people will not have to pay bribes to collect what they are entitled to.

A second unifying solution to the issue of corruption is the imposition of term limits for government officials. Incumbency confers a lot of power on politicians and political appointees to the point that many become consumed by such power and pay no attention to the needs of the people they are supposed to serve. Taking a look at some African countries, one can see the effect of indefinite possession of power on the corruption level in these countries.

The latest example is that of former Gambian president Yahya Jammeh who was forced out of the country by ECOWAS troops in January 2017. Jammeh had ruled the country for over 20 years and was alleged to have stolen and mismanaged a total sum of about $1 billion. Other modern corrupt long-serving leaders include Robert Mugabe of Zimbabwe (who has been ruling for 30 years) and the late Mobutu Sese Seko of Democratic Republic of Congo. Term limits ensure that people can hold a political leader accountable within the period of service. It also restricts them from making choices that prolong their career since there is a constitutional limit on the number of years they can serve. In most democracies, the term limit is two, with each cycle spanning four years. Term limits also drastically reduce the chances of politicians holding on to power as it encourages transparency. A new administration can always go back to check the country's books and conduct investigation into financial misconduct. This way, anyone aspiring to any political office will have probity on their minds and will desist from acts of corruption.

Although we can't fully stop corruption, it can be harnessed at a significant level by preventing the use of invisible transactions, dealings, and favors. The cash, connection, and contracts are vital factors of corruption. We need a cashless society to make every transaction visible. Contracts must be visible for accountability, and connections or influence must be monitored. Corruption is not a core value! The practice and execution of core values can put a complete pause on an exploration of other options that lead to corruption.

About the Author

Edwin Masih, the author of *"Core-option"* has a special gift for expressing his thoughts through writing. Sharing his creative ideas or thoughts through a chat or discussions felt limited when it only included a group of friends, co-workers, or social gatherings. Curiosity to reach millions made him speak his mind through a book. An ordinary person with an interesting journey from India to Indiana, he never had a silver spoon, and nothing fell in his lap; but he believes that if you want to reach your destination, "Walk, don't talk." On his blog, he says, "Don't follow the brand or a trend, you be the brand or a trend."

Currently he is working as a nurse practitioner with America's leading brain and spine surgery group, Goodman Campbell Brain and Spine, Indiana. U.S. welcomed him as an immigrant in 2001. He arrived with his wife and two daughters, and later, his son was born in the U.S. He didn't have much support, there was no job lined up, no apartment contract signed, no credit history. There was only four hundred dollars in his pocket. He didn't turn to excuses for his circumstances, condition, or failure to gain sympathy or to grab attention. Instead, he became a person who inspires and uplift others that have lost their faith, passion and dreams. He writes blogs and quotes to create the "power of words" to build up people.

One of his quotes on corruption:

"Corrupt minds can stop your promotion;
they can never stop your progress."

Email address: *eddiemasih1@gmail.com*